FURTHER ADVENTURES OF A GRUMPY OLD ROCK STAR

FURTHER ADVENTURES
OF A GRUMPY OLD
ROCK STAR

Rick Wakeman

with Martin Roach

preface
publishing

Published by Preface 2009

10 9 8 7 6 5 4 3 2 1

Copyright © Rick Wakeman and Martin Roach, 2009

Rick Wakeman and Martin Roach have asserted their right to be
identified as the authors of this work under the Copyright,
Designs and Patents Act 1988

First published in Great Britain in 2009 by Preface Publishing
20 Vauxhall Bridge Road
London SW1V 2SA

An imprint of The Random House Group Limited

www.rbooks.co.uk
www.prefacepublishing.co.uk

Addresses for companies within The Random House Group Limited
can be found at www.randomhouse.co.uk

The Random House Group Limited Reg. No. 954009

A CIP catalogue record for this book is available from the British Library

ISBN 978 1 84809 175 7

The Random House Group Limited supports The Forest Stewardship Council (FSC),
the leading international forest certification organisation. All our titles that are
printed on Greenpeace-approved FSC-certified paper carry the FSC logo.
Our paper procurement policy can be found at www.rbooks.co.uk/environment

Mixed Sources
Product group from well-managed
forests and other controlled sources
www.fsc.org Cert no. TT-COC-2139
© 1996 Forest Stewardship Council

Typeset in Fairfield by Palimpsest Book Production Ltd,
Grangemouth, Stirlingshire

Printed and bound in Great Britain
by Clays Ltd, St Ives PLC

CONTENTS

SIGNINGS

Let me tell you about Bob Flett and his wooden leg. Life out on the road in a rock 'n' roll band is full of practical jokes. When I do my one-man show it's a fairly modest affair with only four crew but they *love* to play tricks on me. Often, when I arrive at a dressing room, there's always a few letters and mementoes to sign; one of the crew's favourite tricks is occasionally to write a fake fan letter. These are always very easy to spot because they're invariably ridiculous. One particular night we were at the Theatre Clwydd in Mold and I was sitting on my own in the dressing room opening a few of these letters. One of them was from a certain Mrs Flett.

> Dear Mr Wakeman,
> I thought you'd like to know how much your music has played a part in the lives of my husband and I. Bob had a very bad sporting accident many, many years ago and has suffered great pain with his leg ever since. So much so that for some time now he has been desperate to have his leg amputated ...

Oh, this is good, this is one of the crew's best-ever letters ...

At first, Mr Wakeman, the hospital would not let him have it amputated because it was not considered to be life threatening. However, because Bob was in so much pain, they eventually agreed to do the operation. One of the most precious things to him is your music, so he insisted that the hospital actually pipe some of your albums into the operating theatre as his leg was amputated . . .

By now I'm howling, this is definitely their funniest one yet . . .

Bob chose various songs from The *Aspirant* Series and specifically highlighted one particular piece because it was ideal for the exact moment when his leg came off . . . so we look forward to hopefully meeting you afterwards, where Bob can show you some of the artificial legs he's had the design of your album covers painted on.

This was genius. I stood up and went out to the backstage area to find the crew and congratulate them on their creative writing. My tour manager at the time was Mike Holden so I found him and said, 'Nice one, Mike, this is an absolute cracker!'

'What is, Rick?'

'You know, this letter about Bob Flett and his leg . . .'

'Not me, Rick – I'd love to take the credit if it's that good but it isn't me. Besides, it's not my handwriting.'

'Well, who was it? Doom? Ian? It can't be Malcolm because there are words with more than three syllables . . .'

I went out to the front of house and Doom was soundchecking the keyboards.

'Great letter, Doom, really made me laugh.'

'What letter's that, Rick?'

I went to all of the crew and no one would take credit for this little masterpiece. So I decided to play along with their charade and said nothing more. Then, during the interval of the show, there was a knock on the door and Mike came in, looking a little unsettled.

'Rick, you're not gonna believe this but there's a bloke outside says he's called Bob Flett and he'd love to meet you after the show.'

Admiring his persistence, I played along some more and said, 'Yes, of course there is, Mike, and I'd love to meet *him*. Just the one leg is it?'

Anyway, the show finished and I went out to meet a few fans. Then Mike took me to one side and walked us over to a couple.

'Rick, I'd like you to meet Bob Flett.'

He was for real. There, standing in front of me, was a man who'd had his leg cut off to my music. Put yourself in my shoes (or, in his case, shoe). What do I say?

All I could think of was 'Hello', but Bob, bless him, was absolutely lovely. He immediately started telling me all about his leg, while I stood there in this theatre in north Wales thinking I'd just entered the Twilight Zone ...

'Oh, Rick, it's so nice to meet you in person. I can't tell you how much of a relief it was to have my leg off. It was fantastic. I was in so much pain, I can't tell you. And the actual moment it came off was brilliant, Rick, they were playing your music just like I'd asked and I could almost *feel* the leg when it fell on the floor. One of the nurses almost fainted but I was ecstatic – it was gone, clean off. No more pain, Rick!'

I had to ask the question.

'That's great, Bob. And that bit in your letter about the album covers ...?'

Without being asked, Bob proceeded to roll up his trouser to reveal a full artificial leg, festooned with artwork from *Journey To The Centre of the Earth*.

And, yes, I did sign it.

Bob and Gina his wife became really good friends and Bob now does a lot of work helping kids who are amputees. He is a tremendous source of encouragement for them and I take my hat off to him. He's a very special guy.

Signings are a very important part of a musician's life. Some bands love them, others consider it a waste of valuable drinking time. Well organised they are great. You get to meet the real fans, many of whom have become friends. Badly organised, which basically means being told at the last minute, is a curse. Of course, like many bands, Yes were not immune to such last-minute curses.

The best of the 'Curse of the Signings' was at the now-defunct Tower Records on Sunset Boulevard in Los Angeles some time around 2002. I don't think anyone had told Chris (Squire), our bass player we were doing a signing so he had been out for a very long liquid lunch. We all arrived and Paul Silveira, our tour manager said, 'We have a little bit of a problem, Chris is here, but he's basically paralytic.'

It wasn't his fault – no one had told him about the signing – but the fact was that he was barely able to stand, never mind sign anything. We tried coffee and water but all to no avail. He was very jovial though and I tried to help out by giving him a hair of the dog in the form of a nice bottle of Chablis. The Chablis went down very well, and Chris went down very shortly after it.

'Not a great idea, Rick,' one of the band said to me.

We eventually had to start so we went down the stairs into the main part of the store to find about 1,500 people queuing round the block to see us. We sat Chris down and he immediately put his head on the table top and went to sleep. Nothing would rouse him. So we started the signing but people seemed totally oblivious to the snoring and were actually trying to get him to sign their albums.

'Chris, Chris, it's so cool to meet you, could you sign this for me, please?'

We were in stitches. Poor old Chris. I even tried to lift his wrist and shove a Sharpie pen in his hand but I ended up scrawling across the table cloth. Eventually we had to say, 'Chris isn't signing anything today. He's not feeling himself.'

I did have a great deal of sympathy because in my drinking days I had regularly found myself in a similar situation to that in which Chris now found himself.

The best moment, however, was reserved for when Chris woke up.

He had absolutely no idea where he was or why there were 1,500 people queuing in a line and parading past him. Not a problem, he simply put his head back on the table and started snoring again.

Around 2003 we had a phase of signing tits. I don't know where that came from (the phase, not the tits); it was all very bizarre and very 'un-Yes-like'. Needless to say, it did not go down well with the wives and girlfriends.

It all started off somewhere down in California after we'd played an open-air show as part of a big festival. We were all seated on this small stage and the fans came up and had a quick chat, then we signed a few album sleeves and whatnot. Then a somewhat buxom girl stood opposite Jon, who very politely said, 'But you haven't got anything to sign . . .?'

She promptly lifted up her T-shirt to reveal a rather large pair of breasts and said, as cool as you like, 'Sign these!' I wasn't married at the time so I found it all most amusing and couldn't wait to sign. We all signed them, even Steve, although his writing was a little bit shaky. Within minutes, the word had spread and every fourth or fifth woman was hoiking her top up for us to sign her breasts. Chris was probably the most imaginative as he found a way of writing Chris Squire over both breasts and at the same time being able to not have to dot the 'i' in either his forename or surname by using the nipples. An absolute work of art.

* * *

There was a period when I was doing both *Countdown* and *Live At Jongleurs* (an alternative comedy show for ITV), which had the effect of really mixing up my audience and bringing people in to see me who'd never come to one of my concerts before. One particular time I'd just done a show at the Southend Apollo and as usual they set up a table in the foyer so that afterwards I could chat with people and do a little bit of a signing. The 'security' was drawn from the Friends of the Theatre group and the three of them had a combined age of around 248.

Here's hoping it doesn't kick off, then, I thought to myself.

I looked along the line and there were a couple of hundred people in the line but nobody I recognised. Quite close to the front were what appeared to be a mother and daughter and directly behind them a pair of very elderly ladies looking quite bemused. *They must be Countdowners,* I can remember thinking. I made a mental note to have a nice little chat with them when they reached the front of the queue.

Eventually the very attractive mother and daughter reached the desk. The mum was in her late thirties and her daughter was probably in her late teens. When they got to the front, the mum looked a little sheepish and so I spoke first to the daughter.

'How old are you?' I asked.

'Nineteen,' she replied.

'Wow,' I said. 'I wouldn't have thought my sort of music was your cup of tea ...'

'Oh, I mainly like *Live At Jongleurs*, to be honest,' she said, 'but actually I did enjoy the concert. I came mainly for Mum, you see.' Then she turned to her mum and whispered, 'Go on, Mum, ask him.'

'I don't want to,' she said.

'Go on, Mum, ask him,' she insisted.

'No, I don't want to.'

'Well, if you won't,' the daughter said, 'then I will.'

I smiled at the daughter and said, 'Ask me what?'

'Well,' she said, 'you met my mum about twenty years ago at one of your rock concerts.'

It became very quiet in the queue and I went a considerably whiter shade of pale.

'No! Nothing like that,' she laughed.

The queue laughed uproariously.

I laughed somewhat nervously.

The daughter then explained to me that at the concert twenty years ago, I'd signed a pair of her mum's knickers and she carried on by saying 'Mum wondered if you'd sign another pair for old time's sake.'

A little chuckle went down the line and I laughed myself; it was all very friendly and good fun.

'Yes, of course!' I said.

The mum undid her handbag and took out a felt-tip pen. I then waited for her to take out a pair of knickers, but no ... she stood up, promptly undid her belt, unzipped her jeans and dropped them to her ankles, revealing the skimpiest of thongs. Although my hand was shaking a little, I did the best I could and signed my name slowly and methodically. It was not an easy task to accomplish and it took me ages to write my middle name – Christopher!

It was now very quiet in the queue, but the silence was broken by one of the elderly ladies who were next in the queue, turning to her friend and saying, 'Oh dear, Ethel, we don't have to do that, do we?'

Thankfully, they didn't.

Having these more 'mature' fans is wonderful, but can sometimes be one of the most hilarious aspects of my career. Working in Yes as well as on my own solo stuff and the one-man show, plus the *Live At Jongleurs* comedy acts, which I host, and then appearing on *Grumpy Old Men* and *Countdown* means I do get a rather eclectic group of people asking for signatures. The Countdowners are generally a little older than most. One particular lady, well, I'll tell you how old she was: she called me 'young man' . . .

'Young man, I've very much enjoyed your concert tonight.'

'Well, thank you very much, thank you for coming along.'

'I had no idea you played the piano. You're really quite good.'

'Well, thank you very much – I have been playing for a while now.'

'Oh, splendid, well done, you are a talented young man. Have you made any discs?'

'Yes. One hundred and thirty-six.'

Seemingly impressed, she turned to go. But then she looked back at me and said, 'Have you sold all of them yet?'

It's not just knickers or breasts that you get asked to autograph. It can be even more glamorous and rock 'n' roll. Like signing keyboard manuals. Because some of my music is reasonably complex and obviously in the 1970s I was renowned for having pretty state-of-the-art technology on the road, the assumption is made by a certain type of fan that I have some deep passion for the technical side of music. To be honest, I don't really; I have a passing interest because it can help you write and perform better music sometimes, but I'm not a technical person – I just play the piano and keyboards.

A typical signing conversation with one of these techie fans goes something like this:

'Hello, Rick, nice to meet you. Can you sign this, please? It's the ultra-rare manual for the 1971 deleted classic synth, The Bumble Bluebottle Mark 2 – do you know it?'

'Er . . .'

'You know, the analogue module with the calibrated capacitors?'

'Oh, yes, *that* one, very good . . .'

'Well, what do you think of it?'

'A superb machine for its time'

'Really? I thought it was crap.'

And off they go, straight on to eBay no doubt, to buy up some old relic because I had basically endorsed it as the finest rare synth ever built.

Apparently.

Those of you who bought my first collection of stories, *Grumpy Old Rock Star* (still available from all good bookshops, and the odd crappy one too, I suspect), may have even had the misfortune to come and hear me tell some of the stories on the promotional tour I did. I loved doing the literary festivals and found the bookshop events were all highly entertaining. One of my favourites was probably the one in Ely. A lovely man called Robert Topping runs a few bookshops and he is always a pleasure to work with, plus I love his store. (Once I'd finished the tour, I realised I'd spent a fortune on buying other books while waiting to do my own book signings.)

I couldn't see a table in Robert's store but he explained that the signing wasn't going to be in the bookshop itself. I was quite pleased, because I was essentially doing a bit of stand-up and, although my routine isn't exactly full of effin' and blindin', there are quite a few stories that you wouldn't necessarily want your grandmother or any passing child to overhear.

Robert also explained that he'd had to find a bigger venue because the demand for tickets had been huge. 'This is largely due to Ian Rankin,' he explained, 'who did a reading here a couple of weeks ago and told the audience not to miss your evening under any circumstances. Tickets then went like wildfire and we needed to find a bigger place.'

'Great. Where did you book?'

'The Catholic church.'

'You haven't heard me speak before, have you?' I retorted, not a little concerned.

'Oh, don't worry, it will be a lovely evening. And besides, the priest is really looking forward to it – in fact, he'll be sitting in the front row. And you'll be speaking from the pulpit.'

Great.

We walked round the corner to the Catholic church and sure enough, there was the priest sitting in the front row. On the journey over, I'd been thinking through all my stories, trying to work out in advance what I could and couldn't say. Within minutes, I'd realised that I couldn't really do about 95 per cent of my material in front of a priest. So, in the face of certain humiliation, I decided to throw caution to the wind and just do the best I could under the circumstances. I strode up to the pulpit, said hello and then for reasons still unbeknown to myself, launched into a completely different opening gambit to my usual beginning.

'I'm actually a Baptist, but I have been in a Catholic church before, you know,' I started, looking across at the priest. 'Yes, I went in for confession. I stepped into the confession box and the old curtain went back and I said, "Forgive me father for I have sinned."

'"Confess your sins, my son," came the retort from the other side of the confessional box.

'"Last week I had a wild orgy, lasting four days, with seventeen virgins which included the use of handcuffs, whips and vast amounts of melted chocolate."'

(Cue a few uncomfortable shufflings in the church pews.)

'There was a short pause and then the voice on the other side of the confessional said, "I know that voice. You're Rick Wakeman. But you're not a Catholic, you're a Baptist, so why are you telling me this?"

'To which I replied, "I'm telling everyone!"'

The whole church just fell about laughing, no one more so than the priest in the front row. This was like a red rag to a bull so I proceeded to tell some of my most inappropriate jokes, gags and stories. I pretty much got away with everything. It was a very funny evening, probably one of the most enjoyable stand-ups I've ever done.

You never know how many people are going to turn up at a signing. When I was promoting an album called *Silent Nights* I had several signings to do and it was, to be fair, a mixed bag. On one particular day I had two stores to do, the first one in Birmingham and then I was due to race down the M1 for a signing in High Wycombe. The one at the HMV store in Birmingham was fantastic: there were about twelve hundred people and an absolutely massive queue.

The second signing of the day in High Wycombe had, by way of neat contrast, no queue at all. In fact, no people at all. A grand total of zero. A real first. Not one solitary person turned up. It was in Woolworths and they'd made a really big effort, there was a huge table with a lovely red carpet in front of it, there were towering piles of albums ready for me to sign, posters, iced water, there'd been adverts on local radio – it was all perfect.

Apart from the fact that no one had come.

I'd actually phoned my record company on the way down the motorway to ask how many they were expecting in High Wycombe but they'd been evasive and said they couldn't really tell. Sometimes, if the prospects for a signing are looking bleak, record companies might get a 'Rent-a-Crowd' in. If you are not a rich record company, then you'll basically get all the shop's staff to go along at lunchtime to queue up and do exactly the same thing. As the artist, you'll eventually end up recognising these 'fans' in the queue; I've even become quite chatty with some of them, none of whom were remotely interested in my music.

I'd been a little bit ahead of schedule for High Wycombe so I took the manager to one side and said, 'Maybe I'm too early – perhaps you're expecting a late rush?'

'Er, no, we aren't.'

'But are people maybe more likely to come a little later, after work's finished?'

'Probably not, no. Most folk round here just go straight home.'

Great.

'Right,' I said, trying to remain positive, 'how do you normally do with signings?'

'Not very good, really – pretty awful, in fact. I'm not sure people round here really like 'em.'

In the face of adversity, I refused to give in. 'I tell you what,' I suggested, 'I'll go and sit at the table anyway, and let's see what happens. You never know, there might be a mad rush in a minute.'

'I doubt it,' the manager said forlornly.

So I went and sat on my own in the middle of the High Wycombe branch of Woolworths, with a long, empty red carpet in front of me and about two hundred unsold albums behind me. The manager put the record on the shop's tannoy but it didn't even fall on deaf ears of any kind because there weren't any ears in the shop.

Then I saw a middle-aged lady making a beeline for me. She stopped halfway across the store to look at my poster, then continued heading towards me. A punter at last! Normally, a turnout of one would have been a catastrophe, obviously, but somehow, refusing to be beaten and taking my seat at the long table of loneliness regardless of the colossal odds stacked against me, her approach felt like a victory, a vindication of my spirit, a pat on the back for the good old British bulldog.

With possibly my biggest-ever smile and my unused felt-tip pen quivering at the ready, I said hello to this woman as she reached the table.

'Oh, hello, dear,' she replied. 'I wonder, can you tell me where the baby clothes are, please?'

I didn't know where the baby department was, so I got up and went to find the manager. He didn't offer to come over and help her, so I trudged back, took my seat in front of the non-existent queue of non-existent fans and said, 'It's up the back.'

'Thank you.'

'You're welcome.'

As she trundled off to buy nappies or whatever, the manager came over to me and, without a hint of regret for my cringe-inducing predicament, said, 'I'm going to stop doing these. They're a bloody waste of time.'

POSTMAN PAT, OAPS, HELLS ANGELS AND A DOG

Rather than signings, it is the afternoon performance – the matinee – that is the bane of a road crew's life. If you are on tour doing the theatres and you suddenly find there's a matinee going on – the crew *hate* it. We always ask promoters not to book us into theatres where there is a matinee scheduled, but inevitably – either through oversight or deliberately! – we always end up with some clashes.

Take Canterbury and Postman Pat. It was the early 1980s and we were due to play a show in the Marlowe Theatre. I was at a service station on the A2 heading down to the gig with my singer Ashley Holt. We were in plenty of time so we'd stopped for a sandwich when my phone rang. This was in the early days of mobile phones so there was nothing slimline about this model – it was literally the size of a brick with a military-sized antenna. I think the battery life was about eight minutes. Hardly anyone had a mobile at the time so the entire cafe in the service station was looking at me and listening in.

'Rick, it's Doom.' (Doom was my keyboard tech and studio engineer at the time.)

'Listen Rick. We got a problem.'

This in itself was not unexpected. Let me tell you about Doom.

His actual name is Stuart Sawney. He is a lovely guy, really hard-working and excellent at his job but he became known as Doom because his favourite expression is, 'It's all gone horribly wrong!' If you said, 'Isn't this a gorgeous day, look at the sun shining and the blue sky,' he'd go, 'Yeah, but it'll probably rain tomorrow.' So he is universally known as Doom.

Back at the A2 service station.

'Hello, Doom. What seems to be the problem?'

'I'm not happy, Rick, not happy at all.'

'Really? You do surprise me. Why's that, Doom?'

'I'm not happy, Big Ian isn't happy either (Big Ian – Ian Barfoot – was, and still is, my out-front house engineer). Rick, none of us are happy.'

'Okay, Doom, I get that you're not happy. Perhaps you could tell me why?'

'It's Postman Pat, Rick.'

'Right. Perhaps you should start at the beginning . . .'

Doom proceeded to explain to me in his most miserable tone how the crew had arrived at the theatre in the early afternoon only to find there was a matinee show by Postman Pat. Worse still, Postman Pat's gear was all over the backstage area, there was more stuff in the loading bay and the clock was running.

'There's a bright red van on stage and everything, Rick . . .' said Doom.

'And a black and white cat?'

'Yes, Rick, how did you know?'

'Never mind, Doom. Listen, I'm sure you can work something out between you.'

'I don't think so, Rick. Postman Pat has told the theatre he won't be coming off stage until five o'clock at the earliest. That's far too late for us to get loaded in and set up.'

'Okay, but why don't you reverse up to the loading bay and start getting the gear in somewhere backstage while Postman Pat's finishing off?'

'Can't do that, Rick, Postman Pat's bloody great lorry is in the loading bay and they won't move it.'

'All right, let me speak to Postman Pat.'

'He's not here, Rick. They said he's gone over to the hotel, the same one we're staying at.'

'Well, why don't you go and find Postman Pat and ask him if he could kindly arrange for his stuff to be moved a little earlier so we can start loading?'

'I've done that already Rick.'

'And?'

'Postman Pat was asleep in his room and had left strict instructions he wasn't to be disturbed.'

'Well, *somebody* must be around.'

'Yes, Rick. Jess the black and white cat.'

'Okay, so did you ask Jess the Cat if he could kindly organise to have their lorry moved?'

'I did, yes, Rick.'

'And what did he say, Doom?'

'He told me to fuck off.'

I have to admit, I was falling about laughing. God knows what the people at the service station were thinking, hearing half a conversation about Postman Pat, Jess the Cat and some bloke called Doom.

Doom somehow got round the problem and the show went brilliantly. I actually felt sorry for Doom because the whole Postman Pat incident had really stressed him out and he'd done rather well getting it sorted. I took him to one side after the show and said, 'Listen, Doom, you've done very well, superb, that was a mess and you sorted it. You managed to talk some sense into Jess the black and white cat and the show was fantastic. I take my hat off to you.'

With a wicked glint in his eye, Doom said, 'Thanks, Rick. I'd love to be backstage for Postman Pat's next matinee, though!'

'Why? What have you done?'

'Well, let's just say that Postman Pat's bright red van might smell for a few weeks. The dressing rooms were locked all afternoon and we couldn't get in them to use the toilets.'

'You didn't.'

'Might have done.'

'Oh God . . . you wee'd in Postman Pat's van.'

'You'll never know but it could have been worse. Big Ian had a curry at lunchtime and only just managed to contain himself.'

Fast-forward to the opening night of my Classical Connection Tour a few years later. I was due to play in Yeovil at the Octagon Theatre but I was running early so I arranged to play a game of golf with a friend before going to the venue. By the time I got to the sound check, it was Big Ian's turn to square up to a favourite children's character.

'I'm not happy, Rick. Doom's not happy, none of us are, Rick.'

'Why, Ian? What's up?'

'Ever heard of Fireman Sam, Rick?'

'What?'

'There's a matinee, Rick. Fireman Sam. It's full of kids, we can't get anywhere near the stage. Worse still, there's only one big dressing room so you're in there with Fireman Sam.'

It turned out that Fireman Sam and his various friends were all actually frustrated Shakespearian thespians.

We decided to make the most of a tricky situation. We couldn't set up our gear until they'd finished, but truth is, we didn't have much for this particular show and so we decided to make the best of a bad job and booked seats for Fireman Sam's matinee performance. We even bought ill-fitting yellow plastic Fireman Sam hats for a quid each (they were actually made for four-to-six-year-olds and so they perched rather precariously on the top of our heads). Six grown men in bright yellow plastic fireman's helmets then took their seats amongst all the mums and very excited kids, most of whom were also wearing yellow plastic helmets.

It was *hilarious*. The would-be thespians weren't sure if they were at Stratford or Yeovil, if the truth be known. There seemed to be a lot of, 'Alas, poor Yorick, pass me the fire hose' going on and we were in stitches. Fireman Sam was more akin to Fireman Hamlet than to any kids' character. Every now and then among the 'Quick! There's a fire on Pontypandy Mountain!' you'd hear a little snippet that sounded like *Henry V* or *King Lear*. The kids were completely bewildered but didn't seem to mind. They cheered Fireman Sam's every movement and hung on to every sentence, even though none of us understood a bloody word.

At various points, one of the props would explode with a few firecrackers and the crowd would gasp, Fireman Sam/Hamlet would rush to the rescue and save the day, then every kid would clap frantically as if he had actually saved the theatre from burning down. However, towards the end of the show one of the pyrotechnics wouldn't go out and the box it was in actually caught fire. The flames were only about six inches high but Fireman Sam/Hamlet shat himself! He was leaping around the stage shouting, 'Fire! Fire!' but everyone just thought it was part of the show. We were crying from laughter. Eventually, while Sam was dancing round like some sort of deranged elf, a theatre attendant came on with a tiny fire extinguisher and put out the flames in about two seconds. The kids were totally bemused now, they could see this fire but didn't understand why Sam wasn't putting it out. Quite a few were devastated, and more than one shed a few tears.

Then about a minute later, the sound of sirens was heard in the street outside and a real-life fireman stormed on to the stage and sprayed even more foam at the small amount of wispy smoke still coming out of the stage box. Meanwhile, Fireman Sam/Hamlet was standing there, shoulders drooped, head hung in shame. Kids were crying and so were we . . . with laughter!

* * *

To be fair to Fireman Sam, my own live shows are never particularly straightforward. Take the shows for my album *1984*, which I released in 1981. Ahead of the game, you see.

That album was done at completely the wrong time for what was happening in the music business. To record this big extravaganza – a concept album with orchestra, choir and the kitchen sink thrown in for good measure – was a complete misnomer at that time. But fortunately the wonderful Tony Stratton-Smith at Charisma Records hated conformity and absolutely loved the idea, so I wrote and recorded this epic rock opera with the wonderful Sir Tim Rice.

We all agreed that despite our grand designs, it was crucial that the record was promoted with a series of great concerts. The problem was that we genuinely didn't have the money to go out on the road with an orchestra, it just wasn't possible. So we decided to get together a big band and stage a series of shows at the Hammersmith Odeon. My manager, Brian 'Deal-a-Day' Lane, started making some phone calls (you will have already met him if you've read *Grumpy Old Rock Star* – still available all over the country in both good and bad bookshops everywhere as well as online, both paperback and hardback. My publisher asked me to get the plug in). Pretty soon we had a cracking line-up: Steve Harley was coming along to sing, I'd got Kenny Lynch as well, a fabulous big band, a lighting rig to die for plus laser lights, a huge PA, three girl singers called The Lillettes, it had all shaped up very quickly as a really big, loud, bombastic rock 'n' roll event. Everything I could want. So we were all set.

This coincided with a period when I was doing what was incorrectly called 'New Age' music – these gentle instrumental pieces would really fit more accurately in the genre of 'New World' music. I'd been asked to create some new acoustic instrumental material and it was selling really rather well. One album that did particularly well was called *Country Airs* which had a track on it called 'Waterfalls', which was undoubtedly my mum's favourite.

Now, my mum, bless her, she loved all this gentle piano stuff; however, she didn't really like the rock music much at all. Truth be told, she never even liked Yes very much. But to her credit, she always supported me in everything I did, regardless of whether she liked it or not. A true mum.

So imagine my surprise when she phoned me the week before the *1984* shows at Hammersmith.

'Hello, Richard.'

'Oh dear.'

I knew I was in trouble the moment she called me Richard.

'Richard, you never told me you were doing concerts in Hammersmith.'

'Well, I didn't think you'd be interested, Mum.'

'Don't be silly, Of course I want to come to one of the shows, Richard. Luckily I phoned up your manager's office, spoke to the secretary there and she said they'd put twelve tickets to one side for me . . .'

'Twelve tickets? There's only you and Dad and you'll hate it.'

'I've invited ten friends, Richard.'

'Friends?'

'Yes, I'm bringing ten people from the Northolt Old People's home (at the time, my mum worked there as a volunteer). They'll love it. I've even played them *Country Airs* and "Waterfalls" and they just loved it. Well, they said they did anyway. A change of scene, the tinkling piano, it's going to be so nice for them, they don't get out much and it'll be such a treat.'

'Mum, this show is not a piano concert.'

'Well, what is it then?'

'It's the rock opera I wrote with Tim Rice . . . you know . . . *1984*. There'll be my full-on rock band, a brass section, girl singers, a laser light show and it will be very loud – Mum, you can't bring them, they'll die.'

'You mean it's not a piano concert'?

'No, Mum.'

'Well, you'll just have to change it, then.'

'I can't change it, Mum, we've sold out all the shows.'

'Are you sure?'

'I'm sure, Mum.'

'Well, you will have to sort something out, Richard, because they are all coming and the youngest is eighty-two.'

I felt it best not to bring the subject up again in front of my mum and so I concentrated the next few weeks on the preparation of the shows. The day of the first show arrived and all the band and I were in the same dressing room getting changed ready for the show. Then the dressing-room door opened and in walked my tour manager at the time, Funky Fat Fred. He had a huge grin on his face.

'What's amusing you, Fred?' I asked.

'Your mum's here.'

'Is she on her own?'

'Nope.'

'Oh God, how many with her?'

'Living?'

Oh great.

'Come on, you know what I mean.'

'Ten, I think, Rick. Your dad's already found his seat. You do seem to be attracting an older crowd these days,' said Fred, unable to resist.

'Piss off, Fred.'

At that moment, in walked Mum and ten extremely old residents of the Northolt Old People's Home. My band was watching this and they thought it was hilarious – they couldn't wait for any outcome. I could: I'd never had a death at one of my shows before!

The old folks all lined up and, to put it mildly, they were completely bewildered. My mum led me down the line, like the backstage aftershow at some bizarre Royal Variety Performance, and I was introduced.

'Richard, I'd like you to meet Elsie, and this is Rose . . .'

I eventually made it to the last man standing. Almost literally. Albert.

'It's no good talking to me, mate,' he said, rather loudly.

'Oh, really?'

'What?'

'Why's that?'

'Pardon?' He twiddled with something in his ear and then said, 'You'll have to excuse me . . . I'm almost completely deaf. Even with my hearing aid turned up full I can't hear *anything*.'

'You'll have a nice night, then,' I said.

Anyway, I put all this to the back of my mind and did the show. It was *brilliant*. I absolutely loved it, to me it had everything you would expect from a prog-rock concert: epic music, laser lights, a loud sound system, huge sets and amazing lighting – it was fabulous. Afterwards, we were all getting cleaned up in the dressing room when Funky Fat Fred came in again.

'Rick, your mum's here again.'

'Are they all with her?' I asked worryingly.

'Oh, they appear to be, Rick. Shell-shocked, perhaps, but they'd like to have a word.'

So Mum traipsed in again and lined them all up to talk to me once more. I started my way down the line, fully expecting a barrage of criticism. The first lady said, 'Rick, we really enjoyed that. It was wonderful.'

'Really? You're just saying that because you like my mum.'

'No, it was brilliant – the lights, the girls singing, the set, amazing.'

It seemed that they had all actually loved the show! I was so shocked.

'What were those red things zooming around the air?' asked another of the old folks.

'Lasers?'

'Yes, lasers – those are rather fabulous, we liked those.'

'And I haven't heard a drum solo like that since the Glen Miller Band were here in the war . . .' said another.

I chatted with them all for some time and was so relieved. Then I made a very simple and common mistake.

I stood in front of one lady with the compulsory cauliflower haircut and obligatory blue rinse. She was about four foot ten.

'I'm so pleased you enjoyed the show. I would have thought that people your age wouldn't have liked it at all.'

With that, the mood darkened instantly and she walked right up close to me, her nose almost wedging itself in my navel, and started prodding me rather firmly, pushing against me to emphasise her words.

'That's just it, "people our age", you all think when we get to our age that all we want is to be wheeled out in the garden with blankets over us and given endless cups of tea. No wonder we are all bloody incontinent.'

I thought to myself, she's absolutely right. When you get to a certain age, why are you meant to dress in a certain way, behave in a certain way, and only listen to music 'for your age'. It's absolute rubbish.

I was mortified and I apologised. I hadn't intended any offence but I could see why my remarks were insensitive. She gradually warmed up and eventually they all congratulated me again and readied to leave.

At the last moment, a voice at the end of the line spoke.

'I heard everything. I didn't even have to turn it on.'

It was Albert.

Six weeks later, the same ten old folks headed back to Hammersmith Odeon for another show.

This time it was to see Status Quo.

The Classical Connection tour that had seen us fall about laughing at Fireman Sam was just myself on two keyboards and a bass player called David Paton (who'd had a band called Pilot and famously wrote 'Magic' and 'January and February'). David also played acoustic guitar and was a really nice guy, albeit a little backward when coming forward in opening his wallet! But he was Scottish after all!

It was a very popular show and we ran it for about three years, just going round playing small theatres. There are three more stories from the Classical Connection days which I'd like to tell you about. I'll start in York in a theatre at the university. The stage was actually on the floor and the audience was racked up, sloping away from us. We'd been playing a short while and I was just doing an announcement when a student wandered onto the stage – paralytic he was, absolutely rat-arsed. He came over to me and said, 'Do you know where the toilets are?'

I was holding the microphone at the time and so my answer – 'Yes, it's just across there, go out through the red door and there's a corridor on the left' – boomed throughout the entire theatre. The audience were in stitches. The drunk student was so shocked at the volume that appeared to come out of my mouth and looked at me with wide but entirely unfocused eyes, then said, 'Sankyou,' and stumbled off.

I turned to the audience who were obviously still tittering away and said, 'That's one for the book some day.' We started to play but were quickly stopped in our tracks by a banging sound. We looked across the auditorium and this drunken student was trying to go through the exit doors at the side of the stage. The one he was trying was locked but he was pushing and pulling, grunting and slurring. I walked across the stage and said, 'No, not that one, it's down there!' Again my voice boomed out through the house PA.

Eventually he found his way to the toilet and we carried on playing. After the show, I was standing in the foyer signing a few autographs and chatting away when the drunken student staggered up to me.

'I want to thank you,' he said.

'What for?'

'You look just like the man who told me where the toilet was. It wasn't you, but it was a man like you.'

I said, 'But how do you know it wasn't me?'

'Because the man who told me where the toilet was,' he replied, 'had the loudest voice I've ever heard.'

A few months later we were playing another regional theatre and it was all going swimmingly. As we headed towards the interval, I saw a slight commotion at the side of the stage. I looked across and the stage manager was gesticulating at me fairly anxiously. Then, about a minute later, he actually held up a hastily scribbled sign that said, 'KEEP PLAYING!'

We'd finished the normal first half by now, but as smoothly as I could I said, 'Thank you, ladies and gentlemen, but due to a technical difficulty, we are going to extend the first half and we are now going to play "After The Ball", a piece I wrote for a film called *White Rock* . . .' We finished playing 'After The Ball' but still the stage manager was holding up the sign. A further two pieces were played and I was getting concerned as we'd eaten heavily into the repertoire for the second half, and I was bemused as to what the hell was going on, to say the least.

Eventually the stage manager took his sign down and gave me a thumbs-up, so I wrapped up the first half and walked off stage. I went to the dressing room and the manager came in seconds later and said, 'Thank you ever so much – I do apologise. We just had a very tricky situation and we didn't know quite what to do.'

'What on earth was the matter?'

'Well, we always open the bar shortly before the interval is about to start. As we did, this couple came in. They weren't drunk but they'd had a few. They went and sat on the bench seat in the far corner of the bar. Pretty soon there was some fairly heavy petting going on . . .'

Oh dear . . .

'So I went over and asked them to calm down a little but they just ignored me and carried on.'

'And . . .?'

'Well, pretty soon this woman was almost topless and had her hand down the man's trousers and we were only about two minutes from the interval, you see . . .'

'Hence the sign,' I said, trying hard to keep a straight face.

'Yes, hence the sign. By now they were spreadeagled across two round tables and you'd nearly finished the first half. So I went and found your tour manager and explained the problem. He said I had to go to the side of the stage with the sign and then walkie-talkie back to my security man who'd stay in the bar and let me know when they were finished.'

'Good plan, excellent in fact. So how did they get on?'

'Well, I was very surprised, because they lasted the whole of "After the Ball", and the medley from *1984*. In fact, when you climaxed during the last piece . . .'

'Thank you so much for sharing this with me. I think I'm getting the message.'

Although most people were not so moved by The Classical Connection as to make love in the theatre bar, the shows were extremely popular and I loved playing them. Obviously, that was a particular type of show, a certain style of music that attracted a certain type of person. Even the poster made it very clear what to expect – there was a picture of me at a piano and David with an acoustic guitar so it was blatantly obvious this was just a gentle little evening of acoustic-styled music.

On one fateful night, we arrived in a town in the north-east – I have a feeling it was Hull. However, as we drove to the venue, we started noticing posters for our show . . . but it was the *wrong* poster. No acoustic guitars, no gentle piano shots, just photos we'd used for the 'Rick Wakeman and his Band' tour, which was a full-on rock show. Across the bottom of the poster there was a white strip that venues use to write their details down and someone had scribbled that night's show on there.

'David,' I said to my stage companion, 'we have a problem.'

As soon as we got to the venue, I found the promoter lurking somewhere and asked him why he'd put those posters up.

'Because that's all we were sent,' he replied.

Great.

'Anyway, we are really pleased because it's all sold out – it's been very popular.'

'Yes, but maybe that's because people are expecting a rock show. And when the curtain goes up on this expected gigantic rock extravaganza to reveal two keyboards on two little stands and an acoustic guitar next to a chair, do you think it will still be a great night?'

'I hadn't thought of that,' the promoter replied, beginning to look a little pale. 'But I'm sure once you start playing it will all be fine.'

And it would have been . . .

. . . had it not been for the twenty-six Hells Angels sitting in the front row.

Now I've been to a few Hells Angels dos over the years and always found them to be really lovely guys, really nice and really friendly, and boy do they know their music. But this was not the crowd you expected to see at a classical-styled concert. Waiting for our cue to walk on stage we found ourselves peeking through from the side curtain with a very clear view of these Hells Angels in the front row and David, (always very astute and acutely aware of any situation that might arise), said, 'I want to go home. I'm not going out there. If we do, we're dead.'

'We can't go home, David. If you think they're going to be cross when we start playing classical-styled music, how do you think they'll react if we just go home? We've got no choice: let's just go on and try not to get killed.'

We walked on and started playing and sure enough it was quite a rowdy audience and we only seemed to be getting a few ripples of applause. Worse still, as there was no interval I didn't really have much chance to get any audience feedback and see if we were likely to make it out alive. At one point there was a rather unpleasant smell on stage which I believe was the aftermath of David filling his Y-Fronts, or it could possibly have been me. It was all very confusing at the time.

Even though we only had two keyboards and guitar, for the sake of self-preservation we tried to make some feeble gestures towards rock 'n' roll. So for example, we somehow played a few snippets from *Six Wives* and even, don't ask me how, played parts of *Journey*, which if I recall correctly had over two hundred musicians for some of the bigger shows. As we approached the end of the last song, I whispered to David, 'Play the last note, quickly say thanks and bow, then we'll run off.'

As the last notes of the last piece were gently dying away, we duly walked to the front of the stage and took our bows. As I leaned forward, a huge hairy hand grabbed on to my arm in a vicelike grip. I tilted my head up slightly and saw an enormous Hells Angel face inches from my own.

The Hells Angel whispered in gruff tones.

'I'm very disappointed, Rick.'

'Er, really? Disappointed?'

This was not good.

(Either David or I were filling them again).

'Yes, *very* disappointed.'

'Er, well, er, why's that?'

'Because you didn't play "Waterfalls".'

As I've mentioned before 'Waterfalls' was about as gentle a piece of music as it was possible to play; my *Country Airs* album had been rather popular on Radio 2 and had sold well to the New Age, New World market.

'Are you doing an encore, Rick?' asked this giant biker.

'Er, we weren't going to . . .'

'But you're going to now, aren't you?'

So we did.

We played 'Waterfalls' and afterwards the biker came up to me again.

'*Country Airs* is my favourite album, Rick. I loved the show.'

As well as introducing me to a wide variety of people, touring so prolifically has seen me spend more than a few nights in hostelries of wildly varying standards. Over the years I've stayed in everything from the most unbelievable six and even seven-star hotels in Dubai to the most terrifying B&Bs on the planet. And I mean *terrifying* . . . However, there is one hotel that stands out above all the rest. It was a humble B&B in Port Talbot, Wales.

To paraphrase the Carlsberg advert, 'Probably the worst hotel in the world.'

Whenever I used to play the small tours, I hated days off – I just got *so* bored. All there was to do was sit in your hotel room and watch rubbish TV, which usually had a fuzzy picture anyway. I'd see the itinerary and always ask the promoter to fill in any blanks. 'I don't care where we play,' I'd say. 'Just find somewhere, I don't want a day off, I'd rather play than have a day off.' Quite often you'd end up playing theatres who wouldn't even stump up a fee, they'd just offer you a percentage of any takings on the night. I didn't care, so long as I was playing.

Now, it is a harsh reality of rock 'n' roll that any band – whether it's a pub band or a stadium-filling rock act – has certain places where they just don't do the business. Often there might seem to be no logical explanation whatsoever for this lack of interest by the public but the fact remains that every musician has black holes where no one is really bothered. It can be as daft as somebody doing fantastic business in Southport but twenty miles down the road in Liverpool they struggle to sell a single ticket. There are no rules for this and it happens all over the place.

My black hole is Port Talbot.

To make matters worse, there were no half-decent hotels in Port Talbot back then either. I'm sure there are nice places in Port Talbot but we never found them.

On one particular tour, we arrived in Port Talbot ahead of a glorious night playing to a few dozen uninterested punters in some godforsaken tiny theatre. We were booked in to this dishevelled B&B which if I recall correctly – quite hard, given the haze of damp fumes that met us when we walked into reception – it gave itself a rather posh name, something like the Grand or the Royal.

The reception stank, there was so much damp in there. In one corner was a tiny desk with an old Welsh fella sitting behind it looking completely bemused that anyone was actually considering staying in this unspeakably unhealthy dump.

'Who on earth booked us in this shithole?' I said, under my breath.

'I was unaware it had been upgraded,' said Ashley Holt, my singer.

'Surely there is somewhere else nearby where we can stay?'

Apparently not.

My band were not impressed. Not impressed at all. These were battle-hardened, heavy-drinking rock 'n' rollers but even they had their limits.

I was already on the brink of a major crew mutiny and we hadn't even checked in.

'Look, chaps, it's only one night – come on, let's just get checked in and get on with it. We'll be out of here early in the morning.'

Then I turned to the man behind the desk and said, 'Is there anywhere we can get a beer, please?'

'No, mate, sorry.'

'A cup of tea, perhaps?'

'No, sorry.'

Great.

Totally dejected, we all trudged off to our rooms.

They were *far* worse than we'd expected.

The bedclothes on my mattress were actually *wet*.

Not damp.

Wet.

There was a sheen of water on the cloth itself. And it smelled appalling. There was no way I was going to sleep in it – I refused even to sit on it at first.

Each member of the band called my room to complain. For those of you who are aware of my band's constant flatulence, drinking and general debauchery, this gives you some idea of just how disgusting this place was.

Of course, by the early hours I was exhausted so I took a deep breath of damp air and decided to lie down on the bed. First I went into the bathroom and got a manky towel that was at least passably dry, put this on top of the bedclothes, turned the light off (I'm sure I felt a small electric shock as I flicked the switch) and lay down gingerly on the bed. The towel was not thick enough, though, and within minutes I was wet. So I grabbed a jumper out of my suitcase and used that as a makeshift sheet instead.

I lay there for a few minutes and then I heard a tapping noise.

I couldn't work out what it was but it had a relentless marching rhythm. And it was definitely in my room.

I flicked the light back on and looked around. I couldn't see anything at first.

Then I looked down at the skirting board and saw an army of cockroaches streaming from out of a hole in the floorboards and stomping noisily around the edges of the room. There were hundreds of them, literally. It was nauseating. Interestingly though, they did appear to be marching around the skirting board in time! It was quite hypnotic!

I'd had enough of this so I put on my now-wet jumper and stomped down to reception. The old boy was still sitting behind his desk, although now he was wearing his dressing gown.

'Evening,' he said.

'Evening. Look, I'll be honest with you, I'm not entirely happy with my room.'

'Oh dear, what room are you in?'

'Twelve.'

'Really, and you don't like it? Twelve?'

'Yes, twelve,' I said, my impatience rising.

'Well, I am surprised. Why?'

'Well, how about the damp and the unbelievable smell and the health risk this place obviously carries?' I suggested.

'Well, I've never had any complaints before . . .'

'Really? I find that hard to believe'

'Not many people stay here.'

I took a deep breath.

And choked on the damp fumes.

'I've also got hundreds of cockroaches marching round the bloody skirting board.'

'I am surprised . . .'

I was incredulous by now.

'How can you be surprised?'

'Well, the thing is, the cockroaches are normally in room six.'

I slept in the car.

It's not always Hells Angels who surprise you at shows. Take Oscar the dog. He lived in Corby, near Northampton. Or at least we assume he did because he was at the Corby Festival Hall the night we rolled up on our tour. Now, over the years I've been lucky enough to play some pretty large crowds, most recently to 82,000 people in Quebec for the entire rendition of *Return to the Centre of the Earth*. But sometimes the smallest shows can be equally rewarding.

I was doing the one-man show so the crew was minimal and the tour had been going really well: we were loving it and the crowds seemed to enjoy themselves too. The Festival Hall was a lovely venue, not huge but a good size, of about seven hundred and fifty capacity.

I'd played there a few times over the years and we'd always sold out easily so we never bothered with pre-promotion for Corby.

Anyway, when we arrived we were rather baffled to find high fencing all round the venue. The crew went to find out what was happening and eventually my tour manager Mike 'Happy' Holden returned.

'The venue's being closed, Rick.'

'What? You're joking.'

'Nope. It's being closed. To make room for a car park. The show is still on but we are one of the last few engagements, so there's no posters or adverts. They've got Kenny Ball due in and they've just had Joe Brown. But no posters or anything. There's a gap in the fence for the audience to get through but apparently tickets haven't exactly been selling well because nobody knows it's happening and most people think the venue's already closed.'

'How many tickets have they sold?'

'Well, the thing is, Rick, remember that nobody really knows the gig is on and—'

'How many, Mike?'

'Seventy-six.'

Great.

'But most of those sold months ago – they haven't shifted one for weeks.'

Give me strength.

'Could be worse, Rick. They only had nine for Kenny Ball.'

At this point, the theatre manager appeared and was very apologetic even though it wasn't actually his fault. He made the point that those seventy-six people had bought the tickets in good faith and had probably already started their journey to the show.

'Fair enough,' I said, somewhat resigned.

We resolved to play the show and make the best of a bad situation. 'This is going to be pretty hard work, lads,' I said to the crew.

'Harder than you think, Rick,' replied Mike.

'Why? What now?'

'The stage is still set up from the very last performance here, Rick, which was a play. They haven't got the riggers or the budget to dismantle the set so we've got to play the show in amongst that.'

Great.

'And what was the play?'

'No idea, Rick.'

'And so what's the stage set then?'

'It's a graveyard, Rick.'

So we set up in the graveyard in this medium-sized venue, waiting for seventy-six people to turn up. Gradually they dripped into their seats, to be fair looking pretty excited. I wasn't. I was about to sit in a graveyard doing a one-man show in a venue that was, for all intents and purposes, closed down.

Mike Holden said, 'Come on, Rick, it'll be a laugh. Besides, I've got a surprise for you . . .'

'I'm not in the mood for surprises.'

'You'll like this one.'

Intrigued, I walked on stage and stood in front of the seventy-six people scattered around this very empty hall. Just as I began to speak, I glanced down at the front row and sitting there, all alone, upright in his seat, was a white West Highland terrier.

Called Oscar. Apparently.

I pointed at Oscar and said, 'There's a bloody dog sitting down here!'

Oscar looked up and went 'Woof!'

A few people started laughing.

I was in knee deep by this point so I decided to embrace the absurdity of it all and speak to Oscar.

'Hello. I don't know where you've come from but it's so nice to see you in the front row. I don't get very many dogs coming to my shows. What I'll do, as this is a special occasion, I will do the entire performance for you.'

'Woof!'

It transpired that the crew had been in the foyer before the show trying to think up something to lift the atmosphere and make the show a little different. The woman who worked in the box office had Oscar with her and Mike asked her if he was well-behaved. 'Lovely,' she said. 'He'll sit still all day if you ask him.' And so Oscar the West Highland Terrier spent the next two and a half hours in seat A24.

I did the entire show for Oscar. I even sat on the side of the stage at one point while I was actually thinking of all the dog jokes and stories I knew. I just told dog story after dog story, including some extremely risky gags. People were having an absolute ball and the show was *brilliant* fun to perform. As an encore I came on and did 'How Much Is That Doggy In The Window?' in the style of Wolfgang Amadeus Mozart. It was such a hoot.

I came off and a few people headed backstage to chat. Probably the entire audience if truth be known! They were hard-core fans and most of them said it was the best one-man show of mine they'd ever seen. I'd really enjoyed it and at one point I turned to Big Ian and said, 'That was fabulous, fantastic, that's one of the shows I'll wish one day that we had recorded.'

'We did, Rick.'

Big Ian had had the foresight to press the record button on the DAT machine and the evening was preserved for ever.

And so you can buy *A Concert For Oscar* at all good retailers (the same shops that sell *Grumpy Old Rock Star*, so you could kill two birds with one stone), or online at voiceprint.com. Somewhere I have a letter purported to be from Oscar the dog, with a paw mark at the bottom saying how much he'd enjoyed the show. He wasn't the only one – to this day it's one of my best-selling CDs.

CATHEDRALS AND A CASTLE

I do have a strong Christian faith but I am one of those people who like to think that I live in the real world rather than in some fantastical, magical place of make-believe. So unfortunately, terrible things sometimes happen. Sadly, one such terrible thing happened to my dear friend Roy Castle, who as you probably know died from lung cancer – despite him being a non-smoker – brought on from the passive smoke he inhaled while performing in clubs as a brilliant trumpet player and all-round performer for years.

I find that choirs can often provide the magical ingredient for some of the most uplifting, emotional and beautiful music ever written. Naturally, much of that music has religious overtones. This is one of my great loves, writing music for choirs and music that includes choirs. To this end I'd written a special piece called *The Gospels*, which was based on the story of Jesus as told by the four gospels: Mathew, Mark, Luke and John. It was a simple idea but by contrast the composition contained some very difficult music.

I'd needed some money to record this complex oratorio, but the meagre funding I did secure meant that, to be brutally honest, the recording was really poor because I was so very limited with what I could do. In fact, most of it was recorded in a small studio on a boat in Walton-on-Thames. It was not good. Even though I managed to get the wonderful tenor Ramon Remedios to sing for peanuts – because he loved the music so much – we were fighting against the odds and the end result was still a compromise. To make matters worse, the label bringing out the album had experienced financial problems whilst putting together their television campaign. Eventually they went bust and the record pretty much sank without trace. We played the piece live as charitable events a few times at concerts in cathedrals such as Bradford and Tewksbury but that seemed to highlight the shortfalls for me even more. It was so frustrating. People would say, 'What's the matter?' and I'd say, 'It's wrong – the music is not right, there are chunks missing, the whole thing is just wrong, I don't like it.' In fact, after Bradford I came off and said, 'That's it, I'm not performing that ever again.' There are a few vinyl copies of the original recording lying around and they are quite collectable if you can find them! Mind you, if people ever say, 'Rick! I've got a copy!' I always say 'Well, don't play it, because it's terrible.'

I was very good friends with Roy Castle and after he'd already had the terrible diagnosis about his lung cancer he called me up one day to ask if I'd perform at a press launch for his campaign to start a specialist foundation and research facility in Liverpool to beat lung cancer. Of course I agreed, so I went along on the day with my son Adam.

Roy walked into the press conference and smiled warmly at the waiting press pack. Now, before I tell you what happened, let me qualify what I am about to say. I have lots of friends who are journalists – some of them have become really good friends and most are truly genuine people, thoughtful and caring and passionate about their job (in fact, I'm engaged to a journalist who hopefully will be Mrs Wakeman by the time you get to read this). However, there are a very small percentage who are even lower than pond life.

We sat there in this big room listening to questions from the press to this man who was dying from a cancer he had done nothing to deserve. Most of the questions were sensible and necessarily poignant and Roy was as sublimely dignified as ever. Then one particular writer, who shall remain nameless but should be ashamed right up until the day he passes away, said, 'Roy, you are a religious man, aren't you?'

'Yes, I am a Christian,' said Roy gently.

'Well, your god's just given you cancer and he's going to kill you, so what do you think of your god now, then? Eh?'

It was so offensive and I remember shaking in fury at the shame of the man's words. To be fair, every other journalist present looked equally shocked: it was so inappropriate and callous. If I'd been in Roy's position and anyone had asked me that question, I'd have struggled not to jump up and punch him on the nose. But Roy was incredible. Without a flicker of anger, he smiled and said, 'We all wonder sometimes why we are put on this earth, what the reason is that we are here. I certainly have a reason now. I'm going to build this centre, which with luck will prevent maybe thousands of people from getting the same cancer that I have and maybe save many lives. If I hadn't become ill I wouldn't be doing this, so now I know why my god gave me this. So, in so many ways, I am thankful to God.'

All the journalists as one applauded Roy's answer, except for the man who had asked the incredibly insensitive question. He left the room in disgrace.

Roy was an amazing character in so many ways. The reason I'm telling you this is because Roy called me a while later when he was getting really quite poorly and was nearing the end. He'd been out continually fund-raising despite his deteriorating health and had somehow managed to raise money and also the profile of his cause to a super level. He phoned me up and said, 'Rick, I'd love you to perform a concert at Liverpool Cathedral. Would you do that for me?' Of course I said yes straight away.

'I'd like you to play *The Gospels* please. I love that record.'

My heart sank. I wanted to help Roy out, but I didn't want to play a piece that I felt was not right, especially in such important circumstances. I took a deep breath and said, 'Roy. I don't actually play the piece any more as it's got so many things wrong. It's my fault. The budget was low and it didn't have the care and attention it really needed. It wants a complete rethink with new music and new narration. One day, I'll rewrite it properly but it will take a few months to do.'

'Rick, maybe you'd rewrite it for me?'

This was surely an impossible task. I was really worried that I couldn't rewrite it in time for the concert. It was a very long work, with a full choir, a large band of musicians, a narrator and an operatic tenor.

'The problem is, Roy, it's a mess and as I said, it needs a complete rewrite over a few months and I'm not sure I have got enough time.'

'*You* haven't got enough time?' There was certainly a touch of irony in his voice!

His words pierced straight to my heart and I felt quite ashamed, but before I could apologise, his now cheeky voice continued with, 'Rick, how do you think I feel?! I probably won't even be there to witness the concert, although I'll be watching from Heaven's balcony.'

'Roy, of course I will do it for you. The rewrite starts tomorrow.'

Roy Castle died in September 1994, two days after he turned sixty-two. The charity concert in Liverpool Cathedral went ahead and the schedule was so tight for the rewrite that the ink was literally barely dry on the sheet music by the time I had to drive to the concert. It was that close. Over three thousand people came to the cathedral that day and the oratorio was performed beautifully by all who took part. It was a magical, phenomenal night. Afterwards, Roy's lovely widow Fiona came to say hello and I thanked her for having us play and then said, 'This is all Roy's doing. It would have been so lovely if Roy had been here to hear what he made happen.'

'He was here, Rick,' she replied. 'He really was.'

TELLY ADDICT: PART I

I'm a telly addict. I just love the goggle box! My house in Camberley had a television in every room, including the bathroom and toilet. I just love TV. So when I moved to Switzerland in 1976 you can imagine my concern about the quality of TV on offer. Let's face it, as beautiful as Switzerland is it's not exactly internationally renowned for being a global centre of excitement, well not back then anyway. It's a small country and at the time they had TV made by the Italians, the Swiss and the Germans but in the predominantly French region where I lived they naturally mainly watched the French stuff.

I say 'stuff'. What that amounted to was *La Lettre*, which is the French equivalent of *Countdown* (in fact, this show was the original and is licensed to Granada in the UK). I did quite well at that quiz. Even though my French is appalling I found that as long as the words I made up had an 'x' in them somewhere I scored reasonably well.

This was long before the days of Sky+ and there weren't any Blockbusters or video shops yet so viewing options were limited, to say the least. Even personal video recorders were still in their very early days – Phillips made one but it was almost as big as the Swiss house I'd moved in to. Also, the Americans used NTSC as their format, the British and most Europeans used PAL and the French used SECAM (yes, the French just had to be different).

It was a pretty hopeless situation.

However, I was a desperate man so I cooked up what I thought was a pretty ingenious scheme. I bought a Phillips video recorder for my parents and one each for a couple of friends. The deal was that they could keep these video machines as their own – they were presents – but in return I asked them to do one thing for me: video a selection of British TV shows I'd list every week and mail me the tapes. That way I could build up a library of programmes to watch.

In theory that is.

Well, it involved 'pressing buttons' so Mum was struggling straight away; Dad was better but you needed to be aware that if you asked for *Dad's Army*, you'd most likely get *Panorama*. But at least you got *something*. That said, usually not all of it as Dad often mistakenly stopped the recordings before the end of a show. It was a disaster.

My friends were a little better but often their wives would have recorded over the top of what I wanted and so an *Omnibus* programme on the 'living bras' was often what I got instead of the *Match of the Day* that I'd 'ordered'.

Then I discovered a company that seemed to be the answer to all my problems. It was sort of, how can I put it, 'semi-legal'. To be fair, the copyright laws at the time were fairly primitive and hadn't yet taken account of the developing home-recording technology. This company offered a service to expats living abroad where they simply posted you a copy of the *TV Times* and the *Radio Times* (remember there were only four British channels at this point), you'd mark up the programmes you wanted taped and post back your order. Then, later on during the following week, a parcel containing the tape would arrive.

At first it worked a treat. Obviously *Match of the Day* and Sunday's *The Big Match* were essential viewing. So all my mates who loved football would deliberately avoid the results and come round to watch the matches on tape. I'd also got one of the first big-screen tellies, a projector set-up, plus a very serviceable bar, so they'd all pile round and we'd get rat-arsed watching the footy. I also had recorded virtually every sitcom that was currently being aired and over a few months I managed to build up a huge collection.

The company providing this service was really good but I couldn't work out how they were making any money, because they charged hardly anything: it was so cheap.

Then one day I found out.

Bang on time, a tape of *Man About The House* and *Mind Your Language* arrived. I was really looking forward to these as they were two of my favourite sitcoms. I ripped the package open and put the tape straight in the machine.

My first reaction was . . . *Blimey, Richard O'Sullivan isn't wearing very much* . . . not that you could see much of his face.

Ten seconds or so went by . . .

And one of the girls seems to be wearing even less . . .

It got worse. Much worse.

Why is there a donkey in this episode?

And why is she . . .? Ah, I don't think this can be Man About The House *. . . and it's certainly not* Mind Your Language.

Wow, another donkey's just joined in!

I turned the telly off as the penny dropped that this was how this video company made their money. Then a wry smile spread across my face as I also realised that someone out there had ordered a highly pornographic film and had actually received an episode of *Man About The House*. I'd love to have seen the confused looks on their faces!

I thought, *I'll keep quiet about this and see what happens.*

Sure enough, a day or so later I got a phone call from someone at the video company. 'Er, Mr Wakeman, has your video arrived? We think there might have been a mistake so as soon as it arrives, could you send it straight back to us, please?'

I couldn't resist . . .

'Funnily enough,' I said, 'I was going to call you about that. I've had a note from Customs in Geneva who want me to go down and see them for some reason . . .'

You could hear the terrified sound of silence on the other end of the phone. Then the line went dead. And I never did receive another copy of the *Radio Times*.

One of my favourite TV genres is quizzes. Same goes for radio quizzes. However, I'm not exactly renowned on the quiz circuit for my extensive knowledge of popular music. People make that assumption, but in fact I'm useless. It's so widely known in radio and television circles that I am useless that when I go to the filming of *Never Mind The Buzzcocks* they allow me to take along colouring books to pass the time away whilst others are answering the questions – I even took a box of Fuzzy Felts once. However, my worst performances are unintentionally reserved for radio's *Pop Quiz*. I've been on there I think fourteen times, which is the exact same number of times I've been on the losing team. I'm perfectly happy with the situation, I just know it's pointless my even listening to the questions because I never know the answers. Eventually, following a string of particularly appalling perform- ances, one team captain said, 'I don't think I ever want Rick in my team any more – he doesn't know a single thing and we always lose when he's on my side.'

I was still booked for one more appearance so I was quite looking forward to the send-off when the day arrived. The producer took me to one side and said, 'Rick, now we are all aware that your knowledge of popular music is, well, how shall I put this . . .'

'Zero?'

'That's the one. Now, you know we can't give you any of the questions and answers beforehand, but we have tried to gear the questions towards areas that we suspect you may have a degree of knowledge of.

'You'll also be on Helen Shapiro's team, and as you know, Helen is virtually guaranteed to win every time she's a captain of one of the teams in Pop Quiz as she's so knowledgeable, so you'll never have a better chance.'

Brilliant! This sounded liked a great idea. I was going to go out with a bang, for certain. On the day of the recording, I did indeed know a few of the other contestants' questions – okay, one or two – but I was very cleverly kept away from saying anything during the main points-scoring rounds. Then, with perfect comic timing, the last question of the last round fell to me. And the scores were level.

Great.

You could see that the producer, the presenter and the audience were willing me to win. I even think the opposition were mentally spurring me on, it had become such a big thing for me to get a question right.

'Rick, we are going to play you a piece of music and you have to tell us who it's written by and what's the precise name of that piece of music.'

Sounds easy enough.

They played this piece and it *was* something I knew . . . but my mind went blank. I knew the music really well, I was sure I did, but I just couldn't get the name to pop into my head.

'We're going to have to hurry you along, Rick . . .'

I sat there huffing and puffing, trying to recall the answer but to no avail.

'I'm sorry Rick, you've sadly run out of time. I can offer it to the other team and this is to win the quiz: do you know what that piece of music was and who it was written by?'

'Yes, it was "Merlin The Magician" by Rick Wakeman.'

One subject I am reasonably expert on is the *Just William* books by Richmal Crompton. I love them. So much so, in fact, that when I agreed to appear on *Celebrity Mastermind* in January 2009

I chose the books and author as my specialist subject. I'd previously been on a celebrity version of *The Weakest Link* but I preferred the *Mastermind* way of doing these shows because all contestants' charities got their money regardless of the outcome, unlike that other quiz show where just the winner earns his charity some cash.

As you would probably expect, things didn't exactly run smoothly on the day of filming, which was in December 2008. To put it mildly. In fact, by the early hours of the following morning I was in Accident & Emergency with a severe leg injury. But let's start at the beginning . . .

They don't always tell you who else is on these sort of shows and I was delighted to learn that my close friend Ian Lavender, formerly of *EastEnders* but perhaps most famously known as Pike from *Dad's Army*, was also taking part. Ian only lives fifteen minutes away and we see each other often so that was a nice surprise. He was doing 'The life and times of Buster Keaton'. Also on the show was Tim Vine ('Elvis Presley' – Tim was the eventual winner) and Phil Daniels ('Chelsea Football Club in the 1970s').

Ian and I arrived at the studio together and found that everybody had separate dressing rooms, but we ended up in the same one just having a laugh at the fact that neither of us knew anything – between the pair of us we were doomed. We didn't care, the money was going to our charities anyway so it was just a bit of fun. (Good news for my chosen charities: I shared the money between Oldham Cats where I am a patron, The Cats' Protection League and Rose Cottage Cats in Norfolk).

The plan was to introduce the celebs to the audience before the filming started. What happens is you stand backstage while they announce who is appearing and then they introduce each person in turn. We were kept waiting in a very dark corridor, just behind the semi-lit TV studio. As we were walking along this corridor I bumped into the lovely Phil Jupitus, a good friend of mine and a very funny man. We got chatting and so the other three walked on ahead.

They introduced the other three contestants and I could hear them starting to announce me. However, I was still talking with Phil and eventually a stagehand said, 'Rick, come on, you're on!' and opened the door into the bright lights.

It was a bit like going into a tunnel when you're driving. Your eyes don't accustom immediately and your brain gets confused. Well, mine does anyway! I walked in and headed towards the shadowy figures already seated. This involved two steps up on to the raised stage areas.

This would have been bad enough in normal circumstances, but to make matters worse the stage on which I was now stumbling half-blind was made of very sharp, very pointy metal corners.

I missed the steps.

Badly.

All this hopefully explains why, when I tripped up the first step and fell onto one of these super-sharp corners before collapsing in a heap on the floor, I had managed to lacerate my shin in a nine inch L-shape right through to the bone.

I have to say that the pain was absolutely phenomenal. My initial reaction was that I must have broken my leg badly, it was so painful and my leg was going numb. The whole audience gasped – it was really quite a tumble – and then suddenly all these floor managers rushed over to help me.

'I'm okay, it's all right, let's just have a look,' I said, wincing. I rolled up my shredded trouser leg to reveal a very deep, very bloody gash along my shin which was literally pouring with blood. The audience gasped even more.

With a bright red puddle forming on the floor, they called the paramedics, by which time my whole leg had gone completely numb. The paramedics insisted that I should go to the hospital straight away.

'But I'll be there ages: you'll have to reschedule, send all the audience home – it's too much messing about. Just bandage me up, give me a painkiller, I'll do the show and then go to the hospital after.'

They said they couldn't do that because of Health and Safety. 'Look,' I said, determined not to cancel the show and deny my pussycat charities of their much-needed dosh, 'it's my choice, I'm very happy to carry on, let's just do it.' They eventually agreed and gave me some painkillers but I have to admit that, by the time they started filming I was beginning to doubt my bravery as my leg was absolutely killing me. Just before they started, I asked the medics guy when I could have some more painkillers and he said I was allowed just two every two hours.

'How many have you got in your hand?' I asked.

'Eight.'

'That'll do,' I said. I grabbed them off him and took the lot.

So by the time the actual filming rolled, I was heavily band-aged, covered in blood and beginning to hallucinate from a mild overdose of very strong painkillers. I really didn't fancy my chances of winning now. In fact, I can barely remember the programme at all because I was so spaced out. I don't really recall answering any questions and I can't remember much else either, although I have a memory of them mopping up the blood by my chair during the interval. The only bit I do remember clearly is that when Ian Lavender took his seat and John Humphrys asked him his name, I shouted out, 'Don't tell him, Pike!'

The BBC people were very good about it all. As soon as the filming was completed, they helped me to the exit and there was a car waiting to rush me to hospital. The nearest A&E was in Hammersmith, which is a very difficult place for me to visit – I'll tell you why in a moment.

The cut to my leg was so severe that Hammersmith couldn't deal with the extent of the injury as they didn't have the neces-sary staff on at that time of night, so I was put back in a car and driven to Charing Cross Hospital. The doctor there was superb. I explained that I had pretty much impaled myself on the stage of *Celebrity Mastermind* and she was really very helpful. She explained what I had damaged and how she was going to repair the leg. I was still chewing away on as many painkillers as I could get hold of so by now the day was a completely surreal blur of television studios, bleeding profusely in waiting rooms, doctors, taxis, Pike and John Humphrys. I didn't leave Charing Cross Hospital until after 4 a.m. and perhaps, on reflection, I shouldn't have driven home! I could feel my leg for most of the journey, to be fair.

Christmas came and went and in all the festive busy-ness we forgot to tell anyone about the accident, so a few of my friends watched the show when it was screened in the New Year and took the mickey out of me for coming last. 'You'd have come last,' I protested, 'if you'd had blood pouring out of a gaping flesh wound and had had enough painkillers to kill a horse!'

I scored something like seventeen points in total. Not a bad effort, I think, even if I did come last. My particular favourite question was towards the end of my specialised subject when all the first batch of painkillers had really kicked in and I just had this wonderful silly grin on my face when John Humphrys said, 'What keyboard instrument was invented in the second century?' and I said, 'Thank you.'

Let me rewind and explain why Hammersmith Hospital is a very difficult place for me to visit. I've got quite a few associations with the place, one very nice one being the Sparks charity that I've helped over the years. We were responsible for putting in the most amazing scanner in there for newborns, which cost about a million quid but has saved hundreds of babies' lives. I've visited the baby wing as a patron of Sparks on a few occasions. So that's the nice side of Hammersmith Hospital for me.

Hammersmith Hospital has lots of stories surrounding it that involve the building next door, Wormwood Scrubs prison. Back in the 1960s a nurse at the hospital became pregnant and it turned out that the daddy was one of the inmates at the prison. No one seemed to ever agree on how it happened (by that I mean how they met up to do the deed, not how they did the actual deed itself), but it was quite a talking point in the area when I was a lad. I seem to recall the inmate being quoted as saying he only wrote her letters. Well, all I can say is there must have been some amazing lead in his pencil!

For me, however, there is another, very difficult, side of visiting Hammersmith Hospital and it's very tough talking about it, even today. It shouldn't be, but it is. It's the hospital where my father was taken after he died.

Dad was quite young when he died, only sixty-four. It was 26 November 1980. He'd been on his way to work, standing on the platform of East Acton station. He used to leave the house very early in the morning, at about seven o'clock to first go and see my grandma to make sure she was okay, then walk round to East Acton station and travel to Liverpool Street where he worked.

Except that on this particular morning he never made it to Liverpool Street because he had a massive heart attack on the station and died on the spot.

As he'd died in a public place there had to be an autopsy so he was taken to Hammersmith Hospital. I was living in Switzerland at the time but came back immediately upon hearing the news from their neighbour Jack Gilmore, and drove straight to my parents' house to be with my mum.

There seemed to be a lot of paperwork that had to be done and so I went up to Hammersmith Hospital two days later to collect the death certificate and also to find out exactly what had happened.

I went on my own because it would have been far too harrowing for my mum. She was deeply upset and in denial as to what had happened to her beloved Cyril.

Now, before I continue I have to state that I have the utmost respect for doctors, nurses, consultants and surgeons, indeed that respect and admiration also stretches to all the people who work at hospitals. I have seen what they do behind the scenes and I know how committed they are. I also know how overworked they are, bogged down with unnecessary paperwork and bureaucratic nonsense that successive governments force upon them, and that for me, is a national disgrace.

On 28 November, just two days after he'd had the heart attack, I arrived at Hammersmith Hospital and was ushered into a small room where I sat on my own for a while until a doctor came in. I remember it as clear as day – I can still picture the scene: there's something about extreme situations like that which crystallise your memory somehow. The doctor seemed flustered, as if the task he was about to perform had just been thrust upon him. He looked very tired – I suspected he'd been on a very long shift. He had a Tesco bag with him, which he put on the desk.

He sat down and regained a little composure. Then, after introducing himself, he said, 'As you know, your father died at East Acton station. We have done an autopsy which showed he had a massive coronary and if it's any consolation to you he was dead before he hit the ground. We know this because he fell facing forward and broke his nose but there was little or no blood. Also a train was pulling into the station at that precise moment and had a lot of staff doctors and nurses on board who were coming down to the hospital, so he was attended to immediately.'

'Right.' It was all rather a lot to take in.

'And here's some paperwork you need, oh, and you'll need this.' With that the doctor pushed the Tesco bag in front of me, then said, 'I've really got to go now, goodbye,' and left the room.

I stood up and looked into the Tesco carrier bag on the desk.

Inside were my father's wallet and his glasses.

It was horrendous.

That's my dad, I thought. *He's in a Tesco carrier bag, I've been given no time and no help. Absolutely nothing, nothing, and now here's his wallet and glasses in a plastic bag.*

Worse still, one of the lenses in his glasses was broken from the impact of his fall on the hard platform. I stood there thinking about Dad, how he had helped so many people, how he was basically responsible for all the design and building of facilities for the disabled in bathrooms all over the world, an amazing character who had made thousands of people's lives better.

And now two of his most personal belongings had just been dumped in a Tesco carrier bag on a worn-out hospital desk.

I just stood there alone and cried my eyes out. It was so upsetting. I was beside myself so I couldn't go back to Mum's and let her see me like that. I just walked around the streets for ages, then went to a pub and had one brandy and loads of coffees, then walked some more before driving back to Mum's.

In the immediate aftermath I just felt angry. I felt angry that Dad had died so young. I felt angry that I'd lost my dad; obviously people focused their attention on Mum and that was only right, of course, she'd been married for forty-odd years to my dad and was totally devastated, but I felt quite bereft too. *He was my dad.* I was a thirty-one-year-old only child and I was distraught. And of course I felt angry at the way Hammersmith Hospital had treated me.

As time went by, I became friends with quite a few people who work in hospitals, whether by chance or through the various charities I support in numerous ways. So that's how I know how fantastic these people are. That little bit of time and insight allows me to step back from my anger and I'm sure that doctor had had a stinking and probably very stressful day, perhaps he'd had to handle a really bad situation somewhere beforehand. They do have the most difficult jobs and maybe in differing circumstances he may have been more accommodating and understanding. I'll never know.

What I did know was that I'd lost my dad and I missed him terribly.

To this day, I can't take the Central Line train and go through East Acton station, past the exact spot where Dad died. It's really weird, but I just can't do it.

I now have quite an involvement with Hammersmith Hospital through the charity SPARKS, of which I am very proud to be a patron. They have helped finance quite a lot of research at many hospitals including Hammersmith and were involved there with the making and installation of a very unique scanner for babies which has helped save many lives over the last few years.

THE BEAUTIFUL GAME, YEE-HAA!

I love my football possibly even more than I love my telly, although as the years have passed, I think the balance is now changing! Over the years, I've played in celebrity matches, been a director of Brentford, a Chairman at Camberley and I've even owned a team in America (Philadelphia Fury). But perhaps it's best if I start off small-scale and tell you about Marlow Town, George Best and the groundsman's hut.

In the early 1970s, like many clubs at the time, Marlow Town was having financial problems. They were a lovely bunch of people and I'd become friends with many of the faces behind the scenes. They desperately needed to find some money so I offered to arrange a charity football match. At that time I was friends with a lot of professional footballers because Yes had an office in Hillgate Street and in the same building was the headquarters of Ken Adams, one of the very first football agents. He looked after the likes of Alan Hudson, Rodney Marsh, Bobby Moore, Stan Bowles, George Best – some great, great names. Occasionally we'd empty all the desks and chairs from the main office in Hillgate Street and have an indoor five-a-side match! That's how I became friends with people like George Best, Peter Shilton,

Gordon Banks and so on, but before I tell you about Marlow Town, let me tell you a little bit about these pro-footballers that I had come to know.

A lot is said about modern-day footballers, some good and a lot of bad, but I will tell you something about their 1970s counterparts: like George Best at Marlow Town, they were the first celebrities to come along and support a charity event.

These guys were very special. They knew how to play football, have fun when not playing and were always around to help out a good cause.

I remember getting a knock on my door way back in the mid-70s from a relation of the little boy Anthony Nolan, who had leukaemia and they were desperately trying to raise money to bring in a chap from New Zealand whose bone marrow seemed to match that of Anthony's. She asked if I could help and I immediately thought 'Charity Football Match'.

I called all the usual guys from the Top Ten XI such as Chris Quentin from *Coronation Street*, Tony Osoba from *Porridge*, David 'Diddy' Hamilton, Tony Selby and Jess Conrad, to name but a few.

I then needed to find a ground and another footballing friend of mine, Stevie Perryman, suggested Hillingdon Borough who were in the then Southern League and had a really nice ground that held quite a few thousand people. The manager was Jimmy Langley who used to play for Fulham. The club very generously offered me a Sunday for no charge and full use of all the facilities, so I was up and running and a date was set.

I then set about organising the professional ringers. I called Ken Adams. 'You'll have difficulties, Rick,' he said, 'we're nearly at the end of the season and the managers are not going to let their top players play in a charity football match for fear of injury at this time of the season.'

Sure enough, he was right. Every manager refused permission for any of their players to appear. I was distraught. True, I could muster up enough celebrity footballers to field two sides, but I knew the standard would not be good enough to keep a crowd truly happy. I also only had access to two kits that had seen better days, if I'm really honest.

The day of the match arrived and I drove with some trepidation to the ground. It was a really deserving cause and the ground was packed. That made me feel even worse as I felt I was letting them down with what they were about to see on the football pitch.

Most of my celebrity friends had already arrived and were mingling in the changing room waiting for me to bring the kit in – for which I was already thinking up excuses . . . 'Sorry guys, they were put on a boiling wash setting instead of a warm wash and that's why they've shrunk quite a lot and also why the additional red blotches are there as well, plus a pair of the wife's red knickers went in the wash with them and they weren't colourfast' … but I didn't need to say anything because as I walked through the door, Stevie Perryman walked in behind me with a huge holdall bag.

'Hi Rick,' he said. 'This is such a great cause that I'm donating two complete sets of kit from my shop in Hayes for the two teams . . . and I want to play.'

I nearly passed out.

Then over the course of the next ten minutes, in walked Peter Shilton (the England goalkeeper), Mickey Droy from Chelsea, Bobby Moore, Frank Worthington . . . the door kept opening and they just poured in.

'I thought you'd all been forbidden to come,' I spluttered.

'Never got the message,' said Peter Shilton.

'Nor me,' said Bobby Moore with that familiar glint in his eye.

Needless to say, when the teams were announced over the tannoy speakers, the crowd went nuts. It poured with rain, but that didn't matter. The pros didn't hold back either and there were a few tackles that had me worried I can tell you.

They all stayed behind afterwards to sign autographs and from that day onwards, I will not have a word said against footballers.

To me they are very special people and many have become close friends.

And now – back to Marlow Town . . .

From my experience with previous charity games, such as Hillingdon, I knew that you had to always get a few ringers, a few ex-pros and some actual talent, otherwise the crowd would very quickly get bored just watching a bunch of celebs trying their best. You can only watch a celebrity playing football for so long, you've got to have some people in there who can actually play a bit.

I was in the Hillgate Street office telling a few people all about the game at Marlow and by chance George Best was there, listening.

'I'll play, Rick,' said George out of the blue.

'Don't be daft, George, you'll be mobbed!' At this point, George Best was arguably the biggest celebrity – never mind footballer – in the world. And a very serious pin-up to boot. But George was serious and the offer was genuine.

On the day of the match, a large crowd had turned up as the rumour mill about George Best playing had gone into over-drive and even though it was meant to be a secret for security reasons, I think I may have accidentally mentioned it a few hundred times in local pubs and even on the radio if I recall! George did have a reputation for sometimes not turning up, (which on occasions included Old Trafford and playing for Manchester United), but I have to say that in everything he ever did for me (on about a dozen occasions) he was always on time, made a brilliant effort and I considered him a great friend and a lovely man.

George didn't play the entire ninety minutes but when he was on the pitch he completely threw himself into the spirit for things, he ran rings around everybody, scored half a dozen goals in about three seconds and then went off to this massive standing ovation. For Marlow Town it was the coup of a lifetime.

Afterwards we all crowded into the clubhouse. It was heaving, with about five hundred specially selected people in there. You couldn't move, the club was making a shed load of extra money over the bar and it was great. I'm in there looking around and thanking people but at the back of my mind I'm thinking, *Where's George?*

Then one of the senior committee men from the club spoke up (unlike professional clubs that had directors, semi-pro clubs were run by a committee and this gentleman, who will remain nameless for reasons that will shortly become apparent, was very much a senior official). His face was beaming.

'Ladies and gentleman, welcome to Marlow Town, I'd like to thank you all for coming along on this splendid day . . .'

As he continued speaking, a terrible realisation dawned on me.

This particular committee member had an eighteen-year-old daughter.

A very beautiful daughter.

Stunning, in fact.

He worshipped her more than anything on the planet. He cherished her with his life and was fiercely protective of her. The Marlow Town footballers all knew that she was very much forbidden fruit and so kept well clear.

I knew she'd been at the match that day but was now nowhere to be found in the clubhouse.

And neither was George Best.

The world's favourite pin-up who was known, to put it mildly, for having an eye for the girls.

Oh shit.

I could feel the whole wonderfully successful day collapsing around me.

I got one of the back-room boys to scout for George and about ten minutes later this guy came back looking rather pale.

'I've found George.'

'Great! Where is he?'

'He's in the groundsman's hut with the senior committee man's daughter.'

Shit.

At this precise moment, I became aware of said senior committee member addressing me directly over the microphone.

'I'd particularly like to thank Rick Wakeman, who has made a huge effort and a fantastic gesture by helping us arrange this charity fixture.' Round of applause. 'And of course, ladies and gentlemen, we also have a very special player here today who really has made this a remarkable occasion. We have a memento for him as a small token of our appreciation, so if Mr George Best would kindly come forward . . .'

(Crowd erupts.)

After a few moments, when George didn't appear, the applause gradually abated and a steward went up to the man in question and whispered something in his ear. I was terrified: if he found out about what was undoubtedly happening in the groundsman's hut, all our hard work would be wasted.

What he said next did come as somewhat of a shock, I have to admit.

He walked back to the microphone in the middle of the small stage and uttered the following words whilst beaming all over his face.

'Apparently,' he said, 'everything's completely under control. George is actually being looked after by my daughter and I'm told he will be with us in a moment.'

An audible round of coughing and spluttering, intermingled with applause and a few cheers, rippled around the clubhouse, but the now proud father never batted an eyelid. The day was a huge success and the curious incident of George Best, the committee man's daughter and the groundsman's hut was never mentioned again.

I was able to arrange these celebrity football matches because I was a long-standing member of the Top Ten XI celebrity team which spent much of the 1970s and 1980s playing charity fixtures (you can read more about the team in *Grumpy Old Rock Star*; by the way, the hardback ISBN is 978 1 84809 004 0 and the paperback ISBN is 978 1 84809 005 7). How I came to be recruited wasn't exactly out of the pages of any football agency manuals.

In the mid-1970s, I was the owner of two racehorses, who were with the John Webber stable (now run by his son Anthony, after John passed away). One of the horses, Tropical Saint, was running at Windsor in a televised evening race. I was due to be interviewed on the television and so vowed to stay sober until I'd spoken my words of wisdom.

I failed.

I have to be honest: I was completely rat-arsed. I was being invited from tent to tent, from race to race, all suitably oiled by masses of alcohol. I was absolutely ratted. By about 9 p.m. I was lying prostrate on the grass in some small marquee, whilst people just looked down and occasionally tutted before stepping over me.

Then I heard a very strong Irish accent speaking to me.

'Mr Wakeman, I hear you like football.'

I looked up, tried to focus and recognised a man known in the business simply as 'Father'.

'Yesshhh, I do like football, yesshh,' I slurred.

'Would you like to play a game tomorrow at Barnet FC? For the Top Ten XI.'

I belched.

'Ssshhmmashing, yeesshh.'

I woke up the next day in my bed at about 10 a.m. and as I drank my morning coffee I started to have vague flashbacks of this small Irishman leaning over me and saying, 'Do you want to play football, Rick, Rick, do you want to play football?' At first it felt like a dream but that was simply because I'd been so incredibly drunk the night before.

I wasn't sure so I phoned up Barnet FC and asked the receptionist if they had a match on that day. They did indeed: a charity match featuring a host of celebrities who were appearing as the Top Ten XI.

Shit.

I showered quickly, grabbed my football boots and, as you do when you are a twenty-five-year-old rock star, jumped into my flamboyant Mulliner Park Ward Cloud III Chinese Eye Rolls-Royce coupé. I finally found the ground and feeling unbelievably hungover made my way to the dressing room and as I walked in all the other celebs and players stopped talking and just stared at me. I was standing there, painfully hungover, feeling total crap. Death warmed up and with long blond hair straggling all down my back.

One of the TV actors who shall remain nameless looked me up and down and said, 'I don't care how much money he's got, if playing rock music means you end up looking like that I'm sticking with acting!'

I surveyed the dressing room slowly, turned to the Irishman and said, 'Have you got a drink?'

'Vitamin drink?'

'No thanks . . . a large Scotch might do the trick though.'

'Are you going to be able to stand up?'

'I'll be fine, thanks.'

I scored a hat-trick.

I didn't do much else to be honest. I didn't run back to help defend, that was too far to run. I was an old-fashioned goal hanger. I suppose today I'd be described as a cross between Rooney and Ronaldo. (Editor's note: I have spoken to some of his celebrity teammates from that time and after a good deal of thought have come to the conclusion that he actually meant Mickey Rooney and Ronald MacDonald.)

The thing about the Top Ten XI was that, despite being a charity fund-raising idea, some of its matches could get quite violent.

Sometimes you played against the local town team rather than other celebrities and those sorts of players thought it was great fun if they could kick a famous face (or famous arse) up in the air. The most violent matches of all, however, were when we played the priests at Worthing Football Club. They would try non-stop to really to kick you up in the air at every opportunity and then as they stood over your crumpled body on the pitch, they'd say, 'Bless you, my child.' Ten minutes later they'd body-slam you to the ground again, make the sign of the cross and jokingly say, 'How naughty of me. God bless you, my son.'

One day we were playing a particularly violent team of priests. Junior Campbell, the great singer who composed the music for *Thomas the Tank Engine* with Ringo Starr, was in our team and because he was a really talented amateur footballer, was getting a real pasting from these priests: 'Bless you, son', 'God bless you, child' and so on. After about forty minutes, he'd just had enough so after yet another vicious challenge he waited for the priest to start saying, 'Bless you, my . . .' and then Junior nutted him.

Early bath for Junior!

Three more of us – including me – and three priests also got their marching orders; in fact, if the game had gone to extra time there would only have been two goalkeepers left on the pitch.

It's quite a leap from a groundsman's hut to owning an American soccer team so let me take you through that particular period of my life. It was 1976 and the American Soccer League was putting franchises up for sale. Phil Woosnam, the ex-Aston Villa footballer, was in charge of the league and I was one of the eleven people who got involved in buying the Philadelphia Fury soccer franchise.

As you do.

Brian 'Deal-a-Day' Lane was also a member with shares, although I'd lay odds his actual financial contribution was nil! I'm sure his skill at creative accountancy worked wonders – you couldn't help but like Brian!

Most of the other members of the syndicate were American and had very Italian-sounding names. None of them knew anything about football, so they said to me, 'Well, you'd better go and get the team sorted.' So there I was, a twenty-seven-year-old long-haired rock muso going off to buy players for a professional soccer team in America.

Fortunately we had far more money than did the English clubs, plus we offered cars, pensions, houses and other perks, so we could attract some decent names. Generally, the American League appealed to older players who were coming to the end of their main careers and wanted something different and some good pension money, so in this way we were able to sign the likes of Johnny Giles from Leeds, the former Arsenal player Terry Mancini, Alan Ball and Peter Osgood from Southampton, to name but a few. The following season I bought Frank Worthington as well. Brilliant. We then brought in Richard Dinnis as manager, who had previously been at Newcastle.

When it came to the first match of the season, all the players had arrived in Philadelphia except Alan Ball who was flying in on the morning of the first game on the Sunday.

I was living in Switzerland and flew in on the Saturday, arriving in New York for some press I had to do and then drove up to Philadelphia. I got to the hotel around midnight and checked in and as I did, I noticed Peter Osgood, my star striker.

He was leaning across the reception desk in a state of semi-consciousness.

'Peter, what are you doing? You've got a game tomorrow!'

'Rick! How are you? It's great here – what a party they are throwing!'

'What party, Peter?'

'The mayor, Rick, he's done us a great party, it's fantastic!'

'And where's Richard, our manager?'

'He's gone to bed, Rick.'

Peter teetered off and I followed him through some ballroom

doors where I was met by a scene of absolute *mayhem*. It was the party of a lifetime, there must have been about a thousand people in there, all drinking, singing, laughing, dancing, falling over, it was chaos. As I scoured the dark corners and bar areas, I began mentally ticking off all the team members who were in there until I eventually got the full squad (apart from Alan Ball) on my team sheet of 'Absolutely Paralytic FC'. And it was my job, as the twenty-seven-year-old rock 'n' roll monster who'd had three heart attacks at twenty-five and could drink for England, to get everyone to bed. The irony was not lost on me.

On the afternoon of the game, I walked into the dressing room of our magnificent stadium to find Alan Ball red-faced and absolutely ripping strips off the rest of the team. He was properly reading the riot act. 'This is such a fantastic opportunity for all of us: our careers are coming to an end in England, here we are getting great wages, a great future, this is our pension, houses, and you lot are all hungover – this is not a professional way to go about this.' To be fair, they all agreed with him.

I made my way to the directors' box. In front of me sat Jimmy Hill who was the president of the team we were playing, the Washington Diplomats. He turned around, shook my hand, introduced himself and said, 'That's quite a team you've assembled, Rick – we don't hold out much hope today and are expecting a very difficult match.'

With the memory of carrying most of our squad unconscious to bed the night before, I replied, 'Jimmy, take it from me: we're nowhere near bedded in yet. I have to say you're the favourites in my book.'

Jimmy leant even closer to me and semi-whispered. 'I don't think so, Rick. You won't believe this but when I arrived at the team hotel in Washington late last night, the mayor was throwing a massive party for the team and most of them were completely legless.'

'In that case, we're in for a very interesting afternoon,' I retorted.

Before the match started the mayor did this big, triumphant speech saying what a great day it was for Philadelphia. The crowd were going nuts. Then our team staggered on to a huge fanfare, which did nothing to soothe their pounding heads, that was for sure. They looked really exhausted and were still obviously hungover. Terry Mancini later told me that as soon as he ran on the pitch his head started thumping. It was a really sunny, hot day and both teams were seemingly preparing to die.

My particular highlight was the kick-off.

Peter Osgood passed the ball to Alan Ball who chipped it back to Terry Mancini, who – out of force of habit – headed it. It's what central defenders do a lot. They head the ball.

Normally though, they would follow a powerful header by running forward to assist the attack.

This was a slightly different occasion though and upon heading the ball, Terry sank to his knees in obvious pain. You could almost see the little tweetie birds flying round his head. Terry later told me he thought his head was going to explode!

All the Americans around us – who knew absolutely nothing about football, sorry, soccer – were saying, 'Gee, look at that, he hit that ball with his head! That guy is so tough, that must have really hurt, this soccer is a real man's game.' The game was played at just slightly below Sunday School pace and ended in a drab 0–0 draw. We lost the resulting penalty shoot-out 3–0. Welcome to American soccer!

I'd first got involved in US soccer because of Ahmet Ertegün and his brother Nesuhi. Yes were signed to Atlantic in America and we had quite a few dealings with them. They were lovely people, both sadly no longer with us. Anyway, Nesuhi absolutely *loved* soccer. It was his dream to be involved in football in some capacity and he was certainly very knowledgeable. Whenever he came to England he'd go to as many football matches as he could.

On one visit in the early 1980s he came to me looking rather troubled.

'I am so worried, Rick, about your stadiums.'

'What do you mean, Nesuhi?' I asked.

'You see, whilst these old stadiums were fantastic when they were built at the turn of the century, they are now really dangerous.'

'Yes, but that's all right for America, Nesuhi, your teams have all this money to build these fantastic new stadiums.'

'Not true, Rick. They go and get big companies to fund them, sponsor the building, companies like McDonald's or Ford or Chrysler, then the stadium is named after them and it is modern and safe and has all the very best amenities. Half your stadiums are made of wood. You let people smoke in them, you have these old metal railings waiting for people to get crushed if the crowd surges forward and if everyone is standing up, you can't do this . . . it is a matter of time . . . someone's going to die, Rick.'

'I can see what you are saying, Nesuhi,' I replied. 'But that isn't gonna happen, because of the way the English game is run.'

'Then they will have blood on their hands, Rick.'

Of course, at the time sponsored stadiums were almost unthinkable to the English game. It took a needless loss of life at both Bradford and Hillsborough to make our national game come to its senses. Thankfully, things have changed but frighteningly for me, almost without exception, everything that Nesuhi prophesised came true. And not just the tragic concerns he had. The glitz and glamour, the Emirates, the Reebok, the huge TV coverage deals, the cheerleaders, half-time shows, the big screens, the razzmatazz. Nesuhi started it all with his brother at New York Cosmos. Plus they started all these academies for youngsters and also encouraged girls to play. Now the irony is that the USA international side is very highly ranked with FIFA. Back in the 1970s the English press pilloried the American game for doing all this but if you look at the English game in the twenty-first century, the Americans have finally caught up, over thirty years later.

Now, Nesuhi's brother Ahmet loved his soccer too. Along with Nesuhi he owned the New York Cosmos and that remains to this day one of the most high-profile American soccer teams ever. At their peak, the Cosmos were getting 70,000 fans per game – people forget how popular the game became for a while over there. If the more knowledgeable Nesuhi wasn't around, Ahmet would sometimes call me to ask advice about possible new signings and if these players were any good. One day my phone rang and it was Ahmet with just such a question.

'Rick, I've got a chance to buy two players and I need to be quick if I want them. I want you to tell me if they're any good or not.'

'Okay, I'll do my best, Ahmet – as long as I have heard of them, obviously.'

'Okay, great, thanks. The first one is . . . hang on a minute, I've got this written down, Rick, the first one is called . . . Pee- . . . er, Pee-lee.'

'Ah, okay, well, that's actually pronounced Pelé.'

'It's written Pee-lee on my piece of paper.'

'Trust me, Ahmet, it's Pelé.'

'Okay, okay. But is he any good?'

'He's is probably the greatest footballer the world has ever seen, Ahmet.'

'Okay, but according to this, he's getting on a bit.'

'Getting on a bit or not, he can still play.'

'So I should buy him, Rick?'

'Can you afford him, Ahmet?'

'*Of course* I can afford him, Rick.'

'Then buy him.'

Brilliant. 'Who's the other player, Ahmet?'

'It's another difficult name, Rick. It's written down. Franz Beckleybob? Bickleybum? The writing's not very clear.'

'Franz Bickleybum?'

'Yes, it says he played for Germany . . .'

'Oh! Franz Beckenbauer! He was the German captain.'

'Who, Beckleybob?'

'No, Beckenbauer, it's Beckenbauer. He's phenomenal, you must sign him. Can you afford—'

'Rick . . . *of course* I can.'

So he did.

He only went and signed Pee-lee and Bickleybum.

A few weeks later, Ahmet phoned me again and said, 'Rick, I've signed Pee-lee and Bickleybum, they are making their debuts next week. You must come as my guest to the game. And if they are no good I will blame you.'

'Trust me, Ahmet, trust me on this one, they'll be all right.'

And they were. They were sensational and it cemented my friendship with the Ertegün brothers even more.

That's enough about the New York Cosmos, billionaire music moguls and South American soccer gods. Let me tell you how I became Chairman of Camberley Town Football Club.

It was 1982 or thereabouts. My two boys Oliver and Adam were staying with me for the weekend, I guess they were probably about ten and twelve years old respectively. I had a copy of the *Daily Express* and noticed that Camberley Town were at home that Saturday. Now, the ground was literally a two-minute drive from my home so I thought that'd be a great trip out with the boys. So I phoned the club to find out what time kick-off was.

The phone had the engaged tone. I wasn't concerned though because that wasn't not unusual on match days as the local press and radio are always on the phone and clubs get very busy. So I thought I'd just take a chance and go down there. We pulled up at the entrance. Big iron gates with the lettering 'Krooner Park' emblazoned over the top. It looked like a nice little ground. Four huge sets of floodlights at each corner, a nice stand that probably seated three hundred or so and a newish-looking club-house.

On the gate was an old boy sitting in a hut on a wooden chair.

'Afternoon. Can we have three tickets, please? Two kids, one adult,' I asked.

'Yes, mate, it's three quid for adults and two quid for kids, so tell you what, call it a fiver.'

'But it's seven pounds for the three of us, isn't it?'

'A fiver's good enough thanks.'

'If you're sure . . . any programmes?'

'They're fifty pence but I'll throw three in for nothing. I've got hundreds of them.'

'But won't you need them for the crowd?'

'You are the crowd.'

'Oh . . . where do we park?'

'Anywhere you like, mate. Enjoy the match.'

We parked up on an empty strip of grass and went inside the ground to the pitch: it was dead. There were literally only a few people in. The two boys loved it – they went off running around the edge of the pitch, having a great time. I walked up to another really nice old fella who was leaning against a railing.

'Bit quiet, isn't it?' I offered.

'No one comes any more,' he replied and explained the club was about to fold up altogether.

'How is their season going?' I enquired.

'Played seventeen, lost seventeen, goals for: three; goals against: sixty-seven.'

'Well, at least they've scored three goals,' I said chuckling as I spoke.

'Own goals,' he said, without looking up.

He went on. 'There's a very nice man called Roy Calver who tries desperately to keep things afloat almost single-handedly, but he's fighting a losing battle. Nobody wants to play for the side any more – it's just hopeless.'

Anyway, the teams came out and by half-time they were four goals down. It could have been ten. It was absolutely demoralising to watch. I took the boys to the clubhouse for a half-time Coca-Cola and went up to the bar where there was a young girl filing her nails. 'Can I have two Cokes and a pint of lager, please?'

'No, sorry. Lager and Coke's off. We haven't had a drinks delivery for eleven weeks.'

'Okay, how about some lemonade and a Scotch?'

'Sorry, lemonade and Scotch is off. In fact, everything is off.'

I looked up and all the optics and bottles were empty.

'Okay, how about a coffee?'

'Sorry, we can't boil the kettle, the electricity's off as well.'

At that moment a man walked up to my side and introduced himself as Roy Calver. I warmed to this man straight away. It was obvious he loved this club and was certainly fighting a seemingly hopeless battle both on and off of the pitch.

He knew I'd been a director at Brentford and started telling me about all the problems he was having with Camberley Town.

'We're in a spot of bother down here, Rick. This club is my life and I think it's going to close down and that would break my heart. I'm all on my own here. We have a committee but we're just fighting a losing battle. You couldn't come and give us some advice, could you?'

'Who's the team manager?' I asked.

'Me,' he replied.

'And the general manager?'

'Me, as well.'

'The coach?'

'Err . . . ah yes, that's me as well.'

'The chairman?'

'We're about to appoint a new one.'

'And in the meantime, who's acting chairman?'

'Me.'

'When's the meeting?'

'Next Thursday at 7 p.m.'

'Well, I'm in London all day at the accountants but I reckon I can get back for about seven thirty. Get all your books and paperwork together and at least I can have a look. I can't promise anything but I'll try and be helpful and give you any advice I can.'

When I walked into the committee room the following Thursday, the first thing I saw was two old guys swapping duck eggs and home-made wine.

Roy was there with another very well-dressed gentleman who worked in a managerial position at Beechams. He was a local man keen to help, as was the fifth person in the room who had recently taken over a nearby pub in Bagshot.

'Thank you for coming tonight, Rick. We've begun the meeting in your absence as we've a lot to try and get through, but as you're here now, I think it's only right and proper that we start off with a few words from our chairman.'

At which point every pair of eyes in the room turned to look at me.

'Sorry, gents, I don't know who he is . . .'

The chap with the duck eggs looked up and said, 'It's you, Rick.'

'Don't be ridiculous, I've just popped in to try and offer some advice. I'm not the chairman, I haven't been proposed or voted for or anything . . .'

'You have,' he replied. 'We voted you in half an hour ago.'

'You can't do that.'

'We can and we did. It was a unanimous vote. Five to nothing. No abstentions.'

'But how can you vote me in as chairman when I haven't put myself up for election?'

'Roy proposed you and Tom seconded you. It was unanimous.'

I was trying not to laugh it was so ludicrous. Truth be known I was really warming to the idea. I started thinking to myself that their situation surely couldn't be as bad as they made out.

'Surely though,' I said with the best air of company and corporate authority that I could muster, 'I should have had some sort of vote in all of this?'

'He's got a point,' another old boy agreed.

'All right,' said Roy. 'We'll vote again. All those in favour of Rick Wakeman being chairman of Camberley Town Football Club, raise your hand.'

Every hand in the room except mine was lifted.

'All those against.'

My lone hand went up.

Tom, who was taking the minutes, reached for his rubber and appeared to be erasing something in the notes he had already written.

He started writing on top of what had been the vote count of 5–0.

'Five to one' he said as he wrote.

Roy then proudly said, 'Rick Wakeman, you are now officially the chairman of Camberley Town Football Club.'

I'd only been looking through the club's accounts and paperwork for a few minutes when I realised they were in all sorts of trouble. They owed money to everybody: the brewery, the VAT man, the electricity supplier, water, phones, everything. Then as I pored over the papers some more, I realised that despite the club not having paid an electricity bill for months the lights were still switched on and working.

'Er, yes, well, our goalkeeper is an electrician.'

'He's crap too,' I interjected.

'He's crucial to the team though.'

'Why? He let in nine on Saturday!'

'He's the only one who knows how to hot-wire us to—'

'I don't want to know . . .'

It transpired that their downfall had begun during their most successful period. They were once a great side but as they had progressed through the divisions their costs had spiralled and when the money had began to run out the best players left and the upward trend was rapidly and fatally reversed. The club's gates and income didn't rise with what was happening on the pitch and the inevitable debt simply caught up with them.

Fortunately, my accountant at the time – David Moss, who is sadly no longer with us – had been involved with a few football clubs at a semi-professional level. He went to the VAT man and bought the club some time, and he also spoke to all the club's creditors and started to get a little room for manoeuvre.

Then we had two fantastic slices of good fortune. I managed to arrange a charity football game to raise funds for the club featuring a host of stars and we packed three thousand people into the ground and earned enough money to pay off the VAT. Then, a short while later, one of my friends who I knew through Olympus Cameras sponsored the team to the tune of £5,000, which was unheard of at the time in those lower divisions.

So between that and some other monies we'd suddenly brought the club up to date and had even started attracting new players. The following season we got through to the quarter-final of the FA Vase, which we lost at Halesowen. But that cup run was great for the town and great for the club.

I'm told that if you know the right faces at the club you can still get some of the best home-made wine in the south of England and duck eggs are aplenty.

'DO YOU STILL OWN XXXX, MATE?'

One of the nicest things about my job is that I get to go to the most amazing places around the world. I've written about my international travels before (if you've forgotten the ISBN for *Grumpy Old Rock Star* when you go to the bookshop, just ask them to search for 'Wakeman+Rick+Grumpy') but I have to mention Costa Rica, which I've visited three times now. I just love going there: the people there are great and it's a beautiful country.

The very first time I went was with my five-piece rock band to play a big show at a festival. We arrived ahead of our equipment and had three days off while all the gear cleared Customs. The first two days were bliss. We were in a really nice hotel with a swimming pool and various little scenic walks in the gardens; the crew caught up on sleep, everyone ate loads and generally relaxed and caught their breath, a rare treat for any touring musician. Then, on the final day off, my son Adam – who was in his early twenties at the time and playing keyboards alongside me in the band – said, 'Hey, listen up, I've got a day trip all arranged for tomorrow.'

'What?' There was a collective groan from the various much older musicians as Adam explained more.

'I've organised a coach trip to go all round Costa Rica. It's a brilliant itinerary – we leave at seven tomorrow morning.'

'What?!'

'Oh, come on, we have to leave early, it's the only way we'll fit everything in. I've arranged it now, it's all booked, it'll be a laugh.'

I laughed.

'Dad'll pay for it'

I stopped laughing.

'Well, in that case,' said Tony Fernandez our drummer, 'tell us what the itinerary is then.'

'Well, we stop first at someone's home and have a traditional Costa Rican breakfast as their guests . . .'

There was a bit of a groan. This was already sounding like El Cheapo Charabanc Outing par excellance!

'. . . then we head off to the butterfly farm . . .'

'Whoa! Stop right there! A butterfly farm? Adam, this is a rock 'n' roll band!'

'Trust me, Dad, it'll be great. Because after that we go and see this waterfall, which is amazing, it basically just gushes out of the cliff face. Then we go and climb up this volcano, then there's a boat trip down a jungle river to spot poisonous frogs, and then you can go horse riding up the mountains if we have time . . .'

By now all the other guys were saying it could be a bit of a crack, so we all agreed to go. Despite my initial reservations, I was actually really impressed that Adam had gone to such effort so I said, 'Okay, I'll pick up everyone's bill, my treat.'

At 7 a.m. the next morning, an ancient twelve-seater bus turned up at the hotel and this motley collection of world-weary rock 'n' rollers climbed aboard, along with numerous crates of alcoholic beverages for the afternoon.

I have to say, we were all rather excited despite the early start – and so to celebrate, some of the band started drinking as soon as the bus pulled off.

Actually, they all started drinking except for the only teetotaller on board.

Me.

Anyway, we were having a great time straight away. The driver was a nice guy and the day ahead felt really exciting so we all congratulated Adam on his superb organisation.

First off we went to this rather large private house where they'd prepared us a traditional breakfast outside on a terrace. It was *fantastic*. Next stop was the butterfly farm. Now if you had said to me before then that at any point in my life I would have been remotely fascinated by a butterfly farm, I'd have laughed my head off. As it happened, we were there for well over an hour – it was brilliant. It was this giant marquee, like an enormous circus tent with a climate-controlled atmosphere and full of the most weird and wonderful butterflies. The band was captivated, against all the odds, and spent ages in there, particularly dwelling on the world's largest butterfly which was just colossal. However, the band's favourite was the butterfly that took a year to come out of its chrysalis but only lived for twelve hours. That struck a particular chord with the extreme rock 'n' rollers among us!

By now we were having a great time; the next stop was to see this waterfall but Adam warned us that there was quite a precarious drive to get there. The Costa Rican driver explained that the roads were quite rickety but that it should be okay and we would stop to take photographs of the waterfall.

'We will take the photos once we cross the Religious Bridge,' he said.

I didn't like the sound of that one bit.

'What do you mean, the Religious Bridge? Is that something to do with a nearby monastery or something?' I asked.

'Oh, no, sorry, it isn't,' he replied.

'Then why is it called the Religious Bridge?' I queried, rather disconcerted.

'You will find out soon enough – relax, relax, all will be okay.'

We started driving down this increasingly steep slope, slipping and sliding down this incredibly narrow road, then we turned a corner and the road fell even more sharply towards what looked like the world's deepest ravine.

Stretching across the ravine, about eight hundred feet above the rocky floor, was a bridge. It had no sides, despite being barely wider than our bus. Worse still, the bridge started on a sharp bend, so we'd have to carry on down this hill and then at the very last minute turn sharp right, hope the wheels gripped the pot-hole ridden road, and get across somehow to the other side.

We all seemed to realise this at the same time.

'He's going to stop,' said Lee Pomeroy.

'Of course he is,' said Tony Fernandez.

'He isn't,' said Adam.

All eyes averted back to the front to look out of the windscreen at this tiny concrete bridge with no sides that stretched over the ravine.

I felt it was my duty to say something.

'Jesus Christ,' I said.

The driver half turned his head toward me.

'. . . and that's why it's called the religious bridge,' he said chuckling away.

Once we'd traversed the Religious Bridge and our heart rates and blood pressure had come down from the ceiling, and underwear checked for accidents, I said, 'Are there any more Religious Bridges?'

'No, that was the only one. And don't worry, only a few vehicles have ever gone over the edge.'

We didn't ask the driver any more questions after that. Next up was the dormant volcano, which was absolutely stunning. The crater was full of blue liquid sulphur and I have never seen a blue colour like it in my life. The whole spectacle was jaw-dropping.

Then we went off on a boat down this river, a fantastic trip where we saw all sorts of animals including these little tree frogs that looked harmless but were in fact incredibly poisonous. A couple of the guys went off and did horse riding and then we all met up again for this fabulous meal to close the day. Then it was time to head home.

Now, by this stage several of the band were pretty legless. Also, we'd been eating some fairly varied and unusual food all day. So let's just say there was an increasingly unpleasant aroma filling up the bus. By now it was pitch-dark and the Costa Rican roads were so precarious in places that we had to crawl along. I'm telling you, never mind the frogs, the band had some severe poisonous weapons of their own: it was flatulence of the very highest calibre.

Which would have been bad enough but for the fact that all the windows on the bus were fixed. They didn't open. This was due to the heat and it was best to use the bus's rather old, but fully functioning air-conditioning system.

It was a system designed to deal with intense heat. I doubt there was anything in the manual that even mentioned odour.

Some of the wind noises the chaps produced were unreal. And I'm no mean slouch myself when it comes to rear performance. It was superb. I know some people (who really must lead a very boring life) don't find flatulence funny, but to me and the band it was very amusing. It's very British, it's a fact of life: farts are *hilarious*.

However, if you are a tired Costa Rican bus driver on tiny wages, sitting on a dark and dangerous pot-hole ridden road, trying to get home to your kids and wife while ten hairy, drunk British rock monsters attempt to gas themselves to death with anal abuse, then I guess for him . . . it's probably not that funny.

To make matters worse, our fabulous bass player Lee Pomeroy suffered abysmally from phenomenal bouts of wind at the best of times and so with the addition of the local alcohol, the fright of the Religious Bridge plus the unusual food, Lee had now gone on to achieve new heights.

Or depths, depending on your sense of smell.

Suddenly Lee grimaced.

It captured all our immediate attention.

We suspected what might follow and it surpassed all our wildest dreams . . . sorry, nightmares.

Long, loud and frightening was the way that Tony Fernandez described it in the bar later to some people he'd just met. It had shaken Tony to the core, well, all of us really.

The stench was instantly and repulsively sickening – I thought he might even have died – and in such an enclosed space it was just *appalling*. Regardless of the nauseating effect it was having on us all, we were just rolling round with laughter but the Benny Hill, British-seaside toilet humour was completely lost on the poor Costa Rican driver, who was becoming increasingly enraged at the foul-smelling haze filling his vehicle.

It was at precisely this moment, (one-and-a-half minutes after Lee's eruption to be exact) that, just over three miles from the hotel, right in the middle of nowhere, he slammed on his brakes and opened the side door. *Good thinking,* I thought, *he's opening the door and releasing all these gases for the final run home.*

'Get out! All of you, get out now!'

A few of us stifled a laugh but he was deadly serious so we climbed out and let a few bonus efforts off as we did so. *Get it all outside,* he was obviously thinking, another good idea.

Then the bus driver jumped back in his bus on his own, slammed the door shut and drove off.

It was a long, tiring three-mile walk back to the hotel. Suddenly Lee Pomeroy's legendary farting ability didn't seem so funny any more. He kept apologising all the way home but to be fair his smell was merely the final straw – we'd all contributed our own particular fragrance to the coach outing.

I have to say though, even as we fell into our beds exhausted and drunk, with the still-lingering whiff of Lee's world shattering

Lionel* still lingering on our clothes, it had surely become a contender for one of the most rock 'n' roll outings of all time.

This wasn't the first or last time I misjudged or accidentally over-stepped the mark in foreign climes. If you are familiar with the phrase, 'Bruddy hell, he done it again!' from my first book of grumpy tales, then you will know that whenever I travel to foreign climes I will always try to speak a little of the native tongue to my audiences. Even if it's just, '*Güten Morgen*, Berlin!' or some-thing like that. '*Güten Tag*,' I suppose, for a gig, but you know what I mean. It's about making an effort.

One easy way of doing this is to announce the forthcoming songs in the native language; there's always a promoter or PR person around who will write down a simple sentence to say 'This next song is called . . .' in Hungarian or whatever.

Which is all fairly straightforward provided you're not playing a gig in Japan. I don't speak a single word of Japanese, and the alphabet may as well be Egyptian hieroglyphics for all they mean to me. My old friend Mr Udo was escorting me to the venue on this particular night and I asked him to teach me a few words. He tried his best, he really did, but it was just so hard to mimic. In the end, we decided to have a few idiot boards down the front of the stage near the monitors, for me to read off when the moment came. Mr Udo introduced me to one of his Japanese guys called George who was really rather excited at the challenge of writing down these simple sentences on idiot boards for me.

'So, what you wanna say, Lick?'

We worked it all out and to get around the strange alphabet we even had the brainwave to write it all out phonetically.

Sounds like a plan.

It should have worked well, it really should.

[* Lionel . . . Lionel Bart. Cockney rhyming slang.]

George wrote the boards out beautifully. They were all in exact order and he placed them perfectly by the monitors, as agreed. So we were all set.

I knew the Japanese audience would be very appreciative of my efforts and things had gone swimmingly well in-between the pieces when I said simple phrases such as 'Thank You. We will now play . . .' but I was actually really excited at the end the show when I was going to say the big goodbyes and thank yous. There was a capacity crowd of five thousand people, and so after the echo of the last chord of the last piece was dying away I walked up to the microphone and started reading the final board. In my mind I was saying: *Ladies and gentlemen, it's been really nice to be here and I very much look forward to coming back very soon.*

'Size-en-restshoo knee o-ki moo-neno on-nanoko ga-ite, ore wa kanoj-yo no sono moonay to tawa-moo-retay.'

I thought I'd nailed it. I was sure I'd read the phonetics perfectly.

However, the stony silence from the five thousand shocked Japanese faces looking up at me suggested that it might not have all gone to plan.

I thought perhaps my pronunciation hadn't been clear enough, so I said it again.

'Size-en-restshoo knee o-ki moo-neno on-nanoko ga-ite, ore wa kanoj-yo no sono moonay to tawa-moo-retay.'

More silence. A few muffled, embarrassed coughs and the odd laugh. I think I saw one girl faint.

Eventually, after about a minute, we walked off stage to subdued applause.

At the side of the stage was standing a very shocked Mr Udo.

'You velly naughty boy, Lick, velly naughty!' he said.

'Why? The show was great! I know my Japanese farewell wasn't really very understandable, but apart from that it was a great gig.'

'Lick, your Japanese farewell was velly, velly understandable,' said Mr Udo.

'So what was the problem, then?' I asked, confused.

'Lick, you velly naughty to say what you did.'

'Listen Mr Udo, I only said "Ladies and gentlemen, it's been really nice to be here and I very much look forward to coming back very soon".'

'You not say that.'

'Well, that's what I asked George to write down.'

Mr Udo screamed to someone to find George.

George arrived looking very sheepish.

They spoke for a minute in Japanese. Well, Mr Udo did most of the talking. He was not a happy Mr Udo that was obvious.

'What did I say then, Mr Udo?'

Mr Udo turned to face me. 'You say, "There is girl in front row with wonderful big tits and I would love to play with them."'

To which George added, stifling a big grin . . . 'And you say it twice!'

When I was a heavy drinker, I naturally loved going Down Under to tour. The Australians love their drink and I did too – it's a drinking man's country really, barbecues and beer and all that. I was signed to A&M down there via a label called Festival Records. The A&R man assigned to me was a lovely fellow and we got on famously. For reasons that will become blatantly obvious as the story unfolds, I won't use his real name, but simply call him Bruce instead!

On one particular tour in the mid-1970s, on our arrival at the airport Bruce was there waiting for us, looking somewhat shell-shocked. He shook our hands and then said, 'I don't know how to tell you this, Rick, it's really awful . . .'

What on earth's the matter? It can't be that bad surely?

'There's a brewery strike on and all the pubs are dry.'

Oh, good God, it's a disaster.

'Is this for real?' I said, deeply disturbed. 'We are here for two weeks! Surely we can get beer from somewhere?'

He explained that there was some black-market booze and that he'd planned ahead of the strike and bulk-purchased a reasonable stash. I say reasonable, that would be for a normal band, for us it was about two hours' supply. But we were impressed by his preparation, nonetheless. I hastened an emergency meeting with my manager Brian 'Deal-a-Day' Lane.

'Brian, we can't have this! It's a total catastrophe. Two weeks without beer – this is unacceptable. What can we do?' We all racked our brains but the strict controls on illicit booze was making life very hard. Brian then made a suggestion that only a rock 'n' roll manager would ever think of.

'Buy the brewery, Rick,' he said.

Genius! Buy the brewery, hopefully end the strike but if not just get in there and drink ourselves senseless. How could it fail?

We immediately opened up negotiations with my lawyer down there to make inroads into buying the brewery – lock, stock and, most importantly, barrel. At the same time ending the strike and in one foul swoop becoming an Australian hero and drink for nothing for the rest of my life. To be honest, I didn't much care about the first one, but drinking for nothing for the rest of my life . . . well, I still salivate at the thought.

Now the truth is that negotiations never really started as it would have taken weeks to even get to the table to open discussions, but 'Deal-a-Day' Lane was well aware of that and did the next best thing. He phoned all the major newspapers, television and radio stations and within an hour or so the hotel was besieged with cameras, reporters and photographers.

The next morning, emblazoned across the front page of the main newspaper was the headline 'Rick Wakeman to Buy Brewery!' with the sub-line saying 'Could the strike be ended by a Rock Star?' Overnight I sort of became a national hero amongst the male drinking fraternity of Australia . . . Well, that is, all of Australia actually.

I never did buy the brewery, or even get close to it. Two days later, the unions and management got back talking together and the strike was ended. I'd like to think that in some small way we'd acted as mediators to bring the two warring parties together and preserve a good Aussie way of life. Incidentally, the rumour mill chose to completely ignore the fact that I hadn't actually ever bought the brewery so whenever I return to Oz someone will always say, 'Hey Rick, mate, do you still own XXXX?'

Bruce was a great guy but our visits to his country invariably caused him considerable marital strife. His wife was very controlling and always liked him back indoors for 6 p.m. for his tea, not out partying with a bunch of lawless drinking rockers from England. One afternoon we invited him out on a bender but first he took me to one side.

'Rick, my wife doesn't mind me going to your concerts, she's just about used to that because she knows it's my job. But if I just go out on the piss with you I'm in deep trouble.'

'Oh, I see, well, I don't want to cause you any problems, never mind.'

'The problem is, Rick, the record company have said I am not to let you out of my sight.'

By 1 a.m. that night, he wasn't *entirely* conscious when we carefully propped him up against his front door onto his doorstep, but I suspect he was perfectly able to hear his enraged wife screaming at him when she found him later.

About 4 p.m. there was some timid knocking at my hotel room door. Gingerly I got out of bed and looked through the peephole in the door.

I saw Bruce. His face looked all bloated like a goldfish bowl.

I opened the door and immediately realised that it wasn't the peephole that made his face look like a bloated goldfish bowl, his face actually did look like a bloated goldfish bowl.

'Can I sleep on your floor please? She's thrown me out.'

He then emptied the contents of his stomach on the rug just inside the door.

* * *

Two days later, we had a meeting with him and beforehand he said, 'I've been told that if I ever come back home in that state again, the marriage is over. So I'm having a barbecue on Saturday at my home and you can all come – then at least I will know where you are and what you are up to. I am the man of the house, so if I want to invite you I will.'

'Why do you say that?'

'She also said that if I invite you to the house the marriage could well be over.'

We all felt sorry for him so we took his wife some chocolates and flowers and vowed to be on our best behaviour. We arrived there and she was obviously not pleased to see us at all. I always remember his house because it backed onto the airport and he had the barbecue in the backyard. His missus said she didn't like flowers and didn't eat chocolate so that was a bit of a poor start. So we ate all their food, got thoroughly pissed and then left.

Back in those days, I used to wear all these flowing capes on stage (what am I saying . . . I still do!). My wardrobe case was due in Oz the very next morning but for some reason it got held up in Customs. I was really worried because I suppose these capes have become very much a trademark and I really didn't want to have to perform without being dressed appropriately.

I phoned Bruce in a bit of a panic.

'I need to buy a cape.'

'Rick, you won't get one in Australia just like that. It's not possible – no one wears capes.'

'I do.'

'Yes, I know *you* do, Rick, but as a general rule Australians don't wear capes.' He drove round and picked me up and we went straight to a shopping mall. We looked for hours but to no avail and eventually had to leave as the shops were shutting. Still no cape.

Then, as we walked back towards the car, we passed a wedding-dress shop. There in the front window was a glorious long white dress with the most spectacular bridal train. 'A cape!'

'That looks nothing like a cape, Rick – it's a bridal train.'

'Close enough.'

The shop was closed. Disaster.

We found a phone box and called the telephone number on the shop sign and spoke to the owner. Even though the shop was closed, the owner knew that this gown was on sale for several thousand dollars so thankfully he drove straight to the shop and let us in.

'It's a beautiful dress, sir. Would your fiancée like to come in and try it on?' said the very accommodating shop owner.

'It's not for his fiancée,' said Bruce. 'It's for him.'

On the day of the show, we sliced a few rips into the gown and messed with the train a bit so that it made a passable cape and outfit but I've seen pictures of the show and, to be honest, I look like a six-foot-plus rock 'n' roller wearing an ill-fitting wedding dress.

After the big show we took Bruce out for a 'quick half' to thank him. The quick half turned in to a couple of gallons and we didn't get him back onto his doorstep until around 3 a.m. and he was not conscious at all. We headed back to the hotel and I was just settling into bed when there was a knock at the door of my room. I got up and opened the door to find Bruce standing there, just like before, still paralytic, barely able to stand up.

He spoke.

'My marriage is over, it is your bloody fault, and I have got nowhere else to stay.' With that he walked into my room, was sick in roughly the same spot as before and collapsed on the sofa where he fell asleep and started to snore incredibly loudly.

Many years later, I bumped into Bruce on yet another tour of Australia. He was no longer in the record business and, just as he'd said, his marriage had ended that night. I apologised profusely and said we hadn't not intended to cause any trouble.

'Don't worry, Rick, it was the best thing anyone ever did for me. Until the marriage finished that night I didn't realise how miserable I was! I live with a twenty-seven-year-old nymphomaniac now.'

I now consider myself to be a highly successful marriage guidance counsellor.

The mid-1980s was not a good time to be in a prog-rock band. It was about the very last thing that anyone wanted to hear. Punk had taken over everything for a few years, but nearly a decade later things weren't much better. Attendances were poor, there were promoters who would disappear without paying you – it was all very demoralising. In 1985 we'd just done a dreadful tour in America and next up was another trek round Australia. The US had been a disaster – people assume that every tour you do is fantastic but this had been bloody awful. To make matters worse, I was very ill with alcoholic hepatitis, but as yet, didn't know it.

We arrived Down Under and everything was going wrong. Literally, everything that could go wrong did. Looking back, we shouldn't really have been out on the road, everything was conspiring against us; mind you, I've always said that I'd rather be out on tour than sitting at home so I determined to make the best of it.

One particular show was booked miles from the nearest major town at one of the RSL clubs, which are scattered all over Australia. They are fabulous places and I am led to believe they were originally built as ex-servicemen's clubs. They are nothing like the British Legion clubs in the UK as most of them are huge and have great performance areas for all sorts of entertainment, sometimes holding a couple of thousand people or more. They have restaurants, cafés, snooker rooms and dozens of slot machines – known as pokies. Great places, and we loved playing them.

We pulled up at this one club after a two hundred-mile drive and the crew started unloading our gear. We were particularly

Me with the late great
Jack Douglas.

'He's behind you!'
Me as Abanazer at the
hall for Cornwall where I
did my first pantomime.
From left to right: Lisa
Wakeman, Oliver
Wakeman, Abanazer,
Adam Wakeman,
Jemma Wakeman.

At a Heritage Luncheon.
From left to right: Mark Kelly, Jess Conrad, Sue Upton, David Kaufman, David Graham,
Pat Kaufman, me, Rachel, Elaine Dean, Tom Dean, Ian Lavender, Miki Lavender.

With Ian Freeman and David Graham who run the Heritage Foundation. I was an extremely
proud president of the foundation for two years.

A very rare picture from the *Wot's on TV Tonight* tour. From left to right me, Adam Wakeman, Fraser Thorneycroft-Smith.

An early photo of Adam and I performing together on stage.

Well at least Eric Sykes and Dennis Waterman look like golfers!

This is the weight I should be!

A one-off photo of my son Benjamin with my mum shortly before she passed away.

A rare photo of me with my mum (on the right) and her sister Olive.
It was taken at her last birthday party.

It was great having no stomach back then – I could see the ball!

Taken at a sound check somewhere. Don't ask me where though – I estimate I've done about five thousand sound checks!

Believe it or not, there is a 'Yes day' in Philadelphia and this picture was taken at the congressman' house where they threw a party for the band. From left to right: me, Steve Howe, Michael Smerconish and his wife, Chris Squire, Jon Anderson, Alan White

Me and Chris at the same party – everyone else had gone home!

excited as this was the only show of the entire tour that had sold out, so it was a rare beacon of success in an otherwise endless series of disappointments. Then I noticed a guy looking intently over at us. Eventually he walked across and spoke.

'You're Rick Wakeman, aren't you?'

'Indeed. And you are?'

'I'm the manager of the club, g'day. What are you doing here today, Rick?'

'Well, I know we're a little early for the show tonight but we're all travelling together and so we always arrive with the gear, which the crew are unloading as we speak—'

'Er, Rick, the show isn't tonight, mate.'

'What?'

'Your show's next week.'

'No, it can't be – I've got the contract here,' I said. I grabbed my case and pulled out the contract from the agent which said quite clearly that the show was that evening.

'Let me see that, please,' said the manager. He read the date and said, 'Oh, bugger me. You're right, Rick, it does say tonight on the contract. Something's gone amiss somewhere down the line.'

Great.

'Shame, Rick, cos it's sold out, you know . . .'

'Yes, we'd heard.'

'Well, look, there is no other show on tonight, so if you want paying, I suppose you'll have to honour the contract and do the show.'

'But will anyone even know that we are here tonight?'

'Not really, Rick, no. They'll all come next week.'

'And what will you say when two thousand people turn up next week and I'm halfway round Australia playing somewhere else?'

'Good point, Rick.'

'Can you let people know that it's on tonight instead?'

'No chance, Rick. We're miles from anywhere – we don't have a local radio station or anything. There'll be a few in here playing the pokies but that'll be about it.'

We had a band conflab and decided to perform regardless. We were, after all, stuck in the middle of nowhere and none of us ever won on the pokies anyway and we were all enthusiastic, but crap at snooker!

The manager was really pleased.

'Great, Rick. I'll try to round up a few members of staff to come in early but, to be honest, your type of music isn't really that popular round these parts.'

'Cheers.'

To the manager's credit, the dressing room was good and he even put a few nibbles and some cans in there for us. Then our introductory music started and our tour manager told us to get ready by the side of the stage. The intro music reached its crescendo which was our cue to walk on stage to lots of welcoming applause and cheering. We found ourselves doing our normal instinctive waving to the masses, only on this occasion there weren't any masses. On this occasion we walked out on stage to 1997 empty seats and just three people (if I recall correctly they weren't even sitting together!). Our audience was made up of three members of staff who'd been strong-armed into coming into the auditorium by the manager . . .

We played the first half of the show as best we could and then went off for the fifteen-minute interval. When we came back on, two of our audience had left and there was just one person remaining, sitting somewhere near the back. I seem to recall his name was Nathan. I remember this because we asked him if he had a request. He did, and it is not printable.

There was no encore.

You might think that a crowd of three would be my smallest audience ever, but you'd be mistaken. I can beat that – I've played to two. I was living on the Isle of Man at the time and my PA and secretary, Candy, phoned me up and said, 'Rick, I've got a weird one for you.'

'Surely not – go on,' I said, thinking, *When is it ever NOT weird?*

'A man has just phoned and said he wants to book you and The English Rock Ensemble for a corporate gig.'

Great! I thought. Corporate gigs can be good fun and usually pretty lucrative. 'How many people and where?'

'Just him. Oh, and his wife.'

'What?'

'Apparently,' Candy explained, 'he's never missed a single tour of yours in thirty years but the last time you went out he was abroad on business and couldn't get back in time. He was devastated so he said he wants to book you to play an identical show for him and his wife.'

'You're kidding! Does he know how much that will cost?'

The cost of a show was huge but over the course of a tour the expenses could be spread out over many gigs and numerous streams of income. For just a one-off show, it was ludicrous.

'Candy, that's going to be the wrong end of forty grand . . .'

'I know, Rick, I told him . . .'

'And . . .?'

'He wants to book the show. He wants to do it in a hotel – he's got some huge hotel in Manchester booked that has a big ballroom. I know you are thinking that your gear will fill up the ballroom but we don't need much room for the audience as there will only be him and his wife.'

'Look,' I said to Candy, 'phone him up and say I'm very flattered that he likes my music so much, but I can't charge him over forty grand for one gig. I'd love to meet him and he can come to any show on my next tour as my personal guest and we'll go and have a bite to eat afterwards.'

The next day the phone rang and it was Candy.

'Rick, he says he wants you to play the show. He knows the cost and he doesn't mind.'

This was just surreal but I couldn't actually see any reason why we shouldn't play the show. When I told the band they thought I was winding them up. But once I'd explained that I was deadly serious, they thought it was hilarious and as they were being paid their usual rates they didn't really care.

When the day of the show arrived, we rolled into Manchester and the crew had already set up the equipment, PA system and lights in this very splendid ballroom. It was exactly what we had used on the tour. We'd played to three thousand-capacity venues with this rig: it was serious stuff. It was pretty tight for space and right down at the front there was just enough room for two lone chairs. It was a full-on show set up, no expense spared, squashed into this room with a pair of chairs – one of the weirdest sights I've ever come across.

We were introduced to this guy and his wife and they were lovely people, very genuine. He just wanted us to play the exact show that he'd missed. We started playing and he was whooping and hollering, even though there were just the two of them watching, although I got the impression his wife was only there for moral support. The fact that she was reading a book throughout was a bit of a giveaway. He, however, was *totally* into it. We got to the slot for the interval and went off for fifteen minutes, and he duly left the room for a toilet break. Then we came back and there he was sitting next to his wife, waiting for the second half. We played the rest of the show and he clapped and cheered throughout. It was all very surreal but kind of fun.

After we finished the last piece, we all walked to the front of the stage and bowed. He clapped and cheered. His wife turned another page.

We walked out the side doors and he carried on cheering and clapping, and so we went back on and did an encore.

Back down the front again, more bowing, more cheering from

our lone audience member and we went through the side doors for the final time, or so we thought.

Whilst we stood outside the doors in the corridor still trying to come to terms with what had just happened, our benefactor came through the doors. I turned to greet him, fully expecting him to be all full of praise, to be honest. But instead he said, 'Rick, that was brilliant but I understand that at the Sheffield show, which is the one I would have come to if I'd been in the country, you did two encores . . . so could you give me some sort of idea please as to how much longer I have to cheer and holler in there before you come back on?'

He got real value for his money. We did three encores!

I might have inadvertently ended the odd marriage (other people's, that is), but I've also seen a fair few 'rock-solid' partnerships over the years. Being in the music biz they're not always exactly conventional, though.

In my early days of doing sessions in the mid-to-late 1960s, every musician worth his salt desperately wanted to get on what was called a 'Fixer's List'. As a musician you had to be able to sight-read music to a very high standard as well as being extremely accomplished on your chosen instrument and also able to play many differing styles of music.

Fixers booked musicians for recording sessions. When a record company or producer wanted to make a record with session musicians, they'd phone a fixer and say, 'I want a guitar player, bass, drummer and two trumpets' or whatever it was they required, and the fixer would book those musicians who would then turn up at the studio on the day in question.

So from a professional musician's point of view, if you got on a top fixer's list you could be working non-stop at top rates. There were three top fixers around at the time and I was doing sessions for all of them, but one fixer in particular gave me most of my work. He's no longer with us sadly, and so as not to embarrass his family, I'll give him a new name . . . Dave Moggie will suffice, I think.

The problem for me back then was most players on any of the fixers' lists were very experienced, at least in their thirties and often forties and fifties. I was only in my late teens. So the odds were stacked against me as regards getting on a fixer's list, let alone fitting in.

I was fortunate that I was getting a few sessions direct from artists or independent producers and I was keen to work hard and learn from these guys. I began to earn myself a decent reputation.

A few producers who'd used me said they'd mention my name to various fixers if they heard they were looking for new talent. I was still living with my parents at the time and one day I came home and Mum said, 'Richard, we've had a phone call from a Mr Dave Moggie and he said to tell you he's got a session for you.'

I vividly remember tingling all over. This was a *massive* break. Mum had very carefully written down all the details. The session was at Advision Studios in London and was for a top producer. The session was with a big orchestra and I was to play the piano. The session was booked from 10 a.m. to 1 p.m. the following Thursday.

'I don't know where that is, Mum,' I said.

She smiled and just like a true mum said, 'I thought not, so I've looked it up in the phone book for you already. It's in New Bond Street.'

Mum had said to make sure I was on time – well, I arrived in New Bond Street two hours early, at 8 a.m.! There was *no way* I was going to miss this opportunity – it really could be the making of my career. I went and had a coffee at a small café near Bond Street station and sat around for what seemed like an eternity, but when I looked at my watch, it was only 8.30. Time was going so slow. I killed a bit more time then at about nine o'clock I couldn't wait any longer so I walked to the number in New Bond Street that Mum had written down.

When I got there it was a building site.

Literally. A hole in the ground.

My first thought was that someone was playing a cruel trick on me, so I phoned Mum. Fortunately she had Dave Moggie's home telephone number. Obviously I didn't have a mobile phone (they hadn't been invented) so Mum said she'd call him for me, explain the error and for me to call her back in fifteen minutes from the same payphone to find out what he'd said.

At 9.15 I phoned Mum back and she said that Dave had already left for the session but his wife Harriet was trying to get hold of him at the studio for me and get the correct address. I called Mum back again at 9.30 and then 9.45 but there was still no news or an alternative address. Finally, at 10.30 – when I was already thirty minutes late – Harriet phoned Mum and I got to the bottom of it.

Advision Studios had moved a year earlier and the new phone book with their correct address had not yet been sent out. The studio had moved to Gosfield Street but I didn't have a clue where that was. I was now nearly in tears – this was my big break evaporating in front of me. I was already forty-five minutes late for the session, so I ran up to Oxford Street and found a policeman, who luckily knew where Gosfield Street was.

I ran the fastest I've ever ran. I ran through the reception doors at about 11.15 and went straight through to the studio. There, in front of me, frowning and less than impressed, was the conductor and musical director standing at his rostrum in front of a forty-piece orchestra filled with some of the most accomplished session players in the world. All looking at this long-haired, out-of-breath novice who was well over an hour late.

I'd never actually met Dave Moggie before. He stood up and introduced himself (he was also a musician and part of the orchestra) and asked me to come to the control room while the rest of the orchestra took a tea break.

'Rick, one of the most important elements of session work is punctuality. When you only have three hours to record three pieces, you can't just turn up when you feel like it.' I tried to tell him the story behind my late arrival and how I'd actually arrived two hours early, but you could tell he was (justifiably) sceptical. Mainly because he said, 'Whatever your excuse is, it's not good enough. Enjoy the session today because it will be the last one you do for me.'

I was literally in tears.

After he'd left, I found out that my lateness had been particularly problematic as many of the pieces started on the piano, so they'd not been able to record anything. Anyway, the orchestra returned from their tea break and the musical director brought everybody to order and said something like, 'I apologise for the delay in starting, everybody, but we'll do what we can in the short space of time left in this session.' I felt myself squirming in my seat at the piano as I felt forty-plus pairs of eyes glaring at me.

I'm not sure whether adrenalin kicked in or whether my concentration was elevated to a new height, but the first two pieces were recorded on the first take. I guess I was also so far gone in terms of disappointment and dejection that I just relaxed and played the music.

The irony was that at 12.45, fifteen minutes before the session was due to finish, we had all the music in the can and we all left the studio early. I caught the train home, my tail between my legs.

When I got back to my parents', my mum said Dave Moggie had been on the telephone and had left a message for me.

'What's he saying? He can't tell me off any more – he's already done that and he's already said he'll never use me again, so there's really no need to phone up and—'

'Richard, my dear, the very nice Mr Moggie said he'd got home, heard from Harriet about all your efforts to find him and how you'd been two hours early, and realised that you'd told him the truth.'

'Well, that's good but it's not really going to help me, is it?'

'I think it is, Richard: he has just booked you for another six sessions.'

I worked for Dave Moggie non-stop for four years after that, sometimes doing as many as fifteen sessions a week.

Dave Moggie is sadly no longer with us. What a character he was. I really loved that man. He played such a massive part in my musical career and life. He always used to pay everyone on the dot at the end of the session, but when you got your cheque it was always a month post-dated.

If Dave couldn't make the session, or if he had more than one on at the same time in different studios, he'd get Barry Morgan to pick the cheques up from his home to hand out. Barry was one of the great session drummers of all time, a giant of the business.

I was living in a little terraced house in West Harrow when one day I got a phone call from Dave. 'Rick, Barry can't pick up the cheques this morning for the session at Trident Studios, can you be the courier today for me and come round and collect everyone's cheques?' He explained where he lived and I said I'd go straight over. He had a big, beautiful house in Middlesex, but that wasn't where he was sending me. He gave me directions to a maisonette in a north London suburb.

The previous day I'd been rehearsing with a great guitarist friend of mine called Mike Egan, and as we were both on the morning session at Trident, he had stayed at my house so we could travel up for the session together.

No such thing as sat-nav back then, but the trusty A–Z got us there by 8 a.m. and we parked up outside three quite posh maisonette buildings which were evenly placed on a large expanse of lawn.

We got out and there was Dave Moggie mowing the lawn.

Nothing unusual about that, I hear you say, but Dave was doing his morning chore whilst just wearing a long, baggy pair of underpants. He said, 'All right, chaps, go upstairs and have a coffee. Harriet is in the kitchen – I'll be up in a minute and give you the cheques to take.'

Mike and I looked at each either and climbed the narrow staircase to the first-floor maisonette where Harriet stood behind a breakfast bar making coffee.

Nothing unusual about that, I hear you say, but Harriet was doing her morning chore whilst wearing even less than her husband was downstairs in the garden. To put it bluntly, she was bollock naked.

'Hello, boys. Coffee or tea?'

Mike whispered to me in his soft Scottish lilt, 'Sod the coffee, let's get out of here.'

'We've got to pick up the cheques,' I pointed out, also under my breath.

Harriet poured the coffee.

'Milk,' she enquired.

'Oh God, surely not,' Mike muttered under his breath.

We drank the coffee black.

Harriet then brought us some biscuits, quite happily wandering around in the nude in front of us as if it was perfectly normal. Then Dave came up and, without any comment or acknowledgement that his naked wife was in a room with two other men, he said, 'I see you've got coffee, boys. You want toast?'

'Er, no, thanks, we'd better get off actually, Dave, if we could just grab those cheques,' I said, all the time trying to keep my eyes firmly on the ceiling.

'Of course, here you go, they are all ready for you,' said Dave. 'Harriet, where's my hat and coat?'

She told him they were by the door and so he followed us down the stairs of this maisonette, we assumed to follow us out.

However, when we got down by the door we saw that there was a milkman's Express Dairy coat and hat on the coat hook. Dave put them both on, again without any explanation whatsoever, and said, 'Nice to see you, chaps.' And then followed us out of the door.

Totally bemused, we didn't know what to expect next and so we set off slowly toward my parked car. Unable to curb our inquisitiveness we gingerly looked around to see what Dave was doing.

He was standing on the door step of his own maisonette with the door slightly ajar.

We heard Harriet shout down, 'Who is it?'

Dave pushed the door more fully open put one foot inside and shouted up the stairs. 'It's the milkman, love. I've come for my money.'

Harriet's voice floated back down the stairs. 'Oh dear,' she said, 'I haven't got the money to pay you . . .'

'In that case, I'm coming right up,' said Dave and disappeared through his own front door and shot up the staircase.

We drove in silence for a while. 'Did I just see what I think I saw?' asked Mike, nervously.

'You did, mate, and no one should ever know about it. Not until I write my book anyway! This is strictly between you and me,' I replied.

'Agreed.'

We parked up in Soho and walked round into St Anne's Court which is just off of Wardour Street. Barry Morgan had just arrived too.

'Sorry I couldn't get over to Dave's to pick up the cheques,' he said. 'I'm grateful to you guys for coming to the rescue. By the way, what did you get this morning? The milkman?'

What alternatives to the milkman there were I never found out, as I never picked up the cheques again.

JEFF CRAMPTON, KEN RUSSELL AND THOR

Jeffrey Crampton is both a brilliant guitar player and a *lovely* guy. However, Jeff is also the most accident-prone man I've ever met. If he was holding a tray of drinks, he'd drop them; if he sat on the arm of a chair it would break. He makes Frank Spencer look like James Bond, but we all love him. Let me tell you a few tales about Jeff.

Mike Egan, who had played guitar on *Journey to the Centre of the Earth* at the Royal Festival Hall, had left the band to go off and tour with Tom Jones and so I needed a replacement guitar player. I hated doing auditions and relied wherever possible on recommendations from musician friends.

Jeffrey came highly recommended as a player who could adapt to all kinds of music and situations. After working with Jeffrey for just one week, we all realised why.

The first meeting was very much a get-together for a chat.

'I'm really looking forward to this,' said Jeffrey.

'And we're really pleased to have you in the band,' I replied.

'So what's the score?' he asked. 'When do rehearsals start?'

'Next Monday,' I said. 'Here's a copy of the *Journey to the Centre of the Earth* album to learn. See you on Monday.'

Jeffrey had an old 1950s Rover, which really suited him. He lived in south London, which from High Wycombe – where we rehearsed – was about an hour's run for a normal person. For Jeffrey it took about three hours due to his getting lost every single time he made the trip.

Monday morning came and one by one the troops arrived for the eleven o'clock start. Jeffrey was one of the last to arrive at a quarter to twelve.

'Sorry chaps. I got lost.'

'If you are prone to getting lost every time you come here,' said Ashley Holt our great singer, 'then you should set off earlier.'

'I did,' said Jeffrey. 'I left at a quarter past four.'

We all settled down in the rehearsal room and prepared to start.

Tony Fernandez started playing the drums.

Roger Newell our bass player started playing.

I started playing.

Ashley started singing.

Jeffrey just sat on his chair holding his guitar.

We stopped.

'Very nice, chaps,' said Jeffrey.

'Thanks Jeff, but it would be even nicer if you joined in with us.'

'I can't,' he said.

'And why not?'

'I don't know the music yet.'

'But I gave you the album to learn over the weekend,' I said.

'I know,' said Jeff, 'but I'm going through a bit of a rough patch with my girlfriend and we had a bit of a row in the early hours of Saturday morning when I got back from here because I was so late . . .'

'Hold on a minute, Jeff. You left here at five thirty.'

'I know. I got lost.'

By now we were all in stitches and couldn't wait for the next part of the adventures of Jeffrey Crampton.

'Well, she shouted at me and then asked me what I'd got under my arm and I said the LP of *Journey to the Centre of the Earth* which I've got to learn and she said, "I don't think so!" walked over to my record player, unplugged it from the wall and threw it out the window.'

'Much damage, Jeffrey?' asked Roger.

'It's a fourth-floor flat,' said Jeffrey.

We spent that day drinking in the Saracen's Head pub in High Wycombe. At another rehearsal Jeffrey arrived with his six guitar cases and we each grabbed one from his car to help him. The cases seemed very light.

'These don't weigh much,' I said.

'No they won't,' said Jeffrey, 'there's no guitars in them. The girlfriend's hid them.'

One summer, Jeff came on tour with me to America. We were due to perform *Journey to the Centre of the Earth* with the New York Symphony Orchestra. On a morning off before one of the shows, Jeff came to see me.

'Rick, you know the very pretty girl who plays in the front desk of the violins. I've asked her if she'd like to come out with me at lunchtime – is that okay?'

'Of course, Jeff. No problem at all. What are you going to do?'

'I'm going to take her to the park and have a picnic.'

'That sounds super, Jeff. Have a great time.'

'I will. And don't worry, Rick, we'll be back in time for the rehearsal.'

About four o'clock that afternoon, the tour manager phoned me up.

'We've got a huge problem, Rick, *huge*.'

'Why? What on earth's gone on?'

'One of our crucially important violinists from the front row violin section is in hospital.'

'Why?' I asked as my mind started to remember something about this woman, Jeff Crampton and a nice day out.

'She went out for a picnic in the park with Jeff.'

'Food poisoning?' I asked.

'No. She fell out of a tree and broke her arm.'

'Hold on. You don't have a picnic up a tree.'

'Apparently Jeffrey does.'

Great.

'Where's Crampton?'

'He's just left the hospital and he's on his way back.'

When Jeff got back to the hotel he looked ever so sorry.

'What on earth happened, Jeff? Last I heard you were going out for a nice picnic.'

'Rick, I'm really sorry. I don't know how it happened. We went to the park to have our picnic, lovely it was, and there was a tree right by where we were sitting. I suggested we should climb up the tree, sit on a branch and look around at all the beautiful flowers and everything in the park.'

'To be fair, Jeff, that sounds like a lovely idea,' I said, momentarily impressed.

'That's what she said, Rick. So she climbed up on the branch and got comfortable. Then I clambered up and sat next to her. It was a lovely view, Rick . . .'

'Yeah, Jeff, I'm sure, but I'm quite keen to know how she ended up in hospital.'

'Well, she moved up so I could fit on the branch, but I couldn't quite fit on so I asked her if she could move along a little bit.'

'And did she?'

'Yes, but there was a problem, Rick.'

'Which was?'

'There wasn't any more branch.'

'What?'

'Yeah, Rick. I looked to my right and she wasn't there any more, she was lying on the ground squealing. I knew she'd hurt herself. We only went for a picnic.'

'That's as may be, Jeff, but you have just single-handedly decimated the balance of the orchestra.'

'I'm ever so sorry, Rick. Shame, it was a lovely view.'

On that very same tour, Jeff shared a room with another band member who shall remain nameless but suffice to say at the time he was single and a hooligan. When I say 'hooligan', I mean a *wonderful* hooligan, a drinking hooligan of the very best kind, with something of a penchant for the ladies. Never fussy though, the only criteria was that they had to have a pulse.

One day Jeff came to me and said, 'I need to move rooms, Rick. I can't take this any more.'

'Why, Jeff? What's the matter?'

'Well, for example, last night I'm having a shower and you know who comes in and I can hear him and he's apparently not on his own. He appears to have a young lady with him. I tried to tell him I was a little uncomfortable about what was happening but he said to mind my own business and get on with my shower. But then he sat this young lady in the sink and was having his wicked way with her.'

I was barely containing my laughter by now, but tried to look serious when I said, 'Oh, okay, well, what did you say, Jeff?'

'I said, "Look, this is not on. I'm in here having a shower."'

'And what did he do?'

'He got a box of matches and set fire to the shower curtain. So now I'm standing there naked in this shower, watching him bonk this bird in the sink. I'm a serious musician, Rick: I need to move rooms and the hot tap doesn't work anymore either.'

Jeffrey eventually moved on when the band was put on hold whilst I was back with Yes; when I did put the English Rock Ensemble back together again, it had a whole new look with a brass section as well as a rhythm section.

* * *

Whilst out on tour in the UK, myself, the drummer Tony Fernandez and singer Ashley Holt were all in a hotel room watching the telly and killing a bit of time one morning. We were channel-hopping and for some reason settled on this rather peculiar kids' programme. There was this women presenter and she'd got all these little two-to-four-year-old kids about sitting round her feet. All innocent and wide-eyed.

'Now, children, we are going to sing a song. Who'd like to do that?'

All these kids clapped and shouted, 'Me! Me! Me!'

'That's great, children, let's do that. Let's sing a song about a farm. And to help us sing the song, Jeffrey is going to play the guitar.'

We all looked across at each other.

Surely not. It couldn't be!

It was.

The camera panned to a lone figure sitting on a stool.

Jeffrey Crampton: rock 'n' roll's rival to Frank Spencer. We were falling about already. We couldn't wait to see what happened. The programme was live. Did the producers have any idea who they had booked?

True to form, Jeff started playing beautifully, as he always did, but then halfway through the song his plectrum fell inside the guitar itself. He actually stopped and said to the presenter, 'I've dropped my plectrum and I can't get it out!' All the kids were looking at him completely bemused. He'd stood up and was shaking his guitar up and down trying to get his plectrum out through the little slits in the sound board. I think it was at that precise moment that Ashley did indeed wet himself.

We were in tears. Eventually he played it without his plectrum then, at the end and with a poker-straight face, he said, 'Well, it would have been much better with a plectrum.'

Then the woman said, 'Now, children, we are going to play a

game called "Pass The 50p", so let's form two teams. I'll be the captain of the girls and Jeffrey, you can be the captain of the boys.'

The kids lined up and started passing a 50p coin over each other's heads and eventually it was passed to Jeffrey who was the last member of the boys' team.

Jeffrey dropped it.

He was now scrambling around looking for it, saying, 'I think it's under the magic tree house . . .'

Ashley wet himself again.

Perhaps the most bizarre Jeff Crampton story was when we were planning to play *King Arthur* on ice. Now, Jeff was quite well known for his phobias. You name it, Jeff had a phobia for it. I'd previously had trouble with Jeff and this show because I'd sent him out in a heavy suit of armour during a video shoot where everybody had to run around like one of the Benny Hill chases. forgetting that he was both asthmatic and terribly claustrophobic. He lasted about two minutes before he fell into a lake.

When I originally did *King Arthur* on ice, ice-skating had not reached the heights of popularity that it went on to attain.

By the 1980s though, ice-skating was big business in the UK. Torvill and Dean had brought the art to a new level.

I decided to try and resurrect *King Arthur* on ice and wanted to take the choreography to a new level. I'd become friends with Robin Cousins through a bass player friend of mine, Chas Cronk (now with The Strawbs) and I'd approached him about doing all the choreography and stage design – if I could get the huge amount of financial backing needed to get the show on the road.

At that time he was putting on a show called *Electric Ice* at a theatre in Victoria and it was just fantastic. He said, 'Come along and see the show, Rick, there's so much you can do with ice these days.'

I went along to the Victoria Palace to see the show and I was really impressed with the set, the choreography, the costumes, the musical score – everything was superb. Very cleverly, Robin had elevated the band above the main stage on a large platform, suspended about fifteen feet in the air.

The show was well under way and I was loving it. I looked up at the platform to see if I recognised any of the band apart from Chas. I didn't. I also couldn't help but notice this sort of strange barricade right in the middle of the platform with the very top of someone's head just barely visible.

I looked at all of the visible band members on the platform and mentally ticked off their instruments: drums, bass, percussion, wind players, but strangely no guitar player. But wait a minute, I could hear a guitar through the PA system. Good player too, and a style that I recognised.

Unmistakably, the guitarist in the middle of this barricade was Jeffrey Crampton.

After the show, I spoke with Robin, congratulated him on the breath-taking performance and the brainwave of suspending a platform for the band to play on.

'Ah, glad you liked that, Rick, although we have had a few technical problems with the guitar player. I believe you know him. Jeffrey Crampton—'

'Crampton! I knew it! Why was he barricaded in?'

'He told me he's worked with you. Good player. Anyway, he's joining us in a minute for a drink. I'll let him tell you because as you know no one tells it like Jeff!'

A short time later, Jeff appeared and I was so pleased to see him. I shook his hand and said, 'Jeff, good to see you, how's things?'

'It's a nightmare, Rick,' he said. 'I love doing the music for this show and I love the band and Robin Cousins is brilliant but we did the rehearsals and everything was going great until he said, "We're going to suspend you in the air." Well, I get vertigo really badly. So I thought, *I won't say anything, I'll overcome it.*'

'Did you, Jeff?'

'No. I was sick on the bass player on the opening night and he wasn't happy at all. In fact, I projectile-vomited, which went a long way and the drummer got hit too. Unfortunately it smelled an awful lot. Probably the curry. You taught me to eat hot curries. Anyway, they came up with the idea that if they barricaded me in. I wouldn't have the sensation that I was actually up in the air.'

'Did it work?'

'No, because the platform rocks quite a lot and it's like being on a boat, Rick.'

'Well, that's okay then,' I said.

'Not really,' he replied. 'I get sea sick you see. I'm not sick as much as I used to be, but one of the other band members says it still stinks.'

Whatever Jeff might have said, done, hit, twisted, fallen off or broken, he remains to this day a legend, a brilliant player highly respected by everyone.

Someone should make a film about him.

Maybe someone like Ken Russell . . . In 1975 I got a phone call from my management saying that Ken Russell wanted me to do the music for a film about Liszt, called *Lisztomania*. I'd never done music for a film before: I knew roughly how to approach it but I was very much a novice. This was going in at the deep end, because Ken had a reputation for being very experienced and knowing exactly what he wanted. It sounded like a serious set-up too, with my manager telling me I'd be assigned a 'music team' of writers and transcribers. Ken also had a reputation for being a very strong-minded character, I was a great Ken Russell fan – I loved *The Music Lovers* and *The Devils* – so it was with degrees of apprehension but mainly genuine excitement that I turned up at Shepperton Studios on my first day.

A lovely man called John Forsythe met me at the studio. 'Welcome, Rick!' he said, 'It's going to be great. Ken knows what he likes, though, Rick – you do know that?'

'I have heard, yes.'

'Right, well, we've already got through something like six music engineers, they don't usually last very long. He likes what he likes, you see.' This wasn't really doing a lot to calm my nerves. Then John took me to meet Ken who was absolutely marvellous. After a little chat, Ken said, 'Now, Rick, I'm delighted you are on board. We have a production meeting every morning at six o'clock sharp. I will require a lot of music – we often shoot film to the music, there's specific pieces we already need and there will be a lot of music I'll need afterwards too. So I'll see you in the morning at six!'

I knew Ken was a stickler for punctuality so the next morning I was there at the production office at two minutes before six. Ken opened the door.

'Morning, Rick! Would you like a drink?'

'I'd love one, please.'

Before I'd had a chance to say 'coffee, white' out came two bottles of white wine.

Ken was such an entertaining man to be around. His reputation for being quite fiery did reveal itself on occasion though, but it was always with the best intentions of making the finest film. One morning he arrived clearly in a foul mood. It later transpired that there'd been an almighty row with financiers and production people behind the scenes and to cut a long story short, it appeared that Ken was now being asked to change parts of the film due to budget.

'They want a changed film, I'll give them a bloody changed film!' Ken ranted.

Then he turned to me and said, 'Rick, now listen: I've done a bit of a rewrite. As you know, we have Roger Daltrey as Liszt; we have Paul Nicholas as Wagner; and now with the rewrite we have Ringo Starr as the Pope.'

No surprises there then.

Not a lot you can say, is there?

'Well, as I've said, I've started the rewrite already. Pretty much the entire film will now be rewritten.'

He continued. 'Now, Rick, tomorrow, we are going to be filming a small mountain on G-Stage. There will be twelve naked girls dancing around, and sitting on top of the mountain will be a man holding the Rheingold. So I need "Ride of the Valkyries" to play whilst filming. The edited version I asked you to prepare. Is it ready?'

'It is, Ken.'

'Good. The scene will be shot to the music. Now because of the nudity, Rick, it will be a closed set – only the actors, you, because you'll be in charge of the music, the crew – and myself of course – will be allowed on set.'

It sounded brilliant so off I went to sort out the music in readiness for the fun and games the next day. Ken wasn't shooting on set until three o'clock so I had plenty of time to check and double check that I had everything sorted for this shoot to music. At 2.30 I walked the short distance from the music department over to the large stage door that hid the closed set. I was let through the door by security and the place was *heaving*. I couldn't move, it was packed solid. There must have been three hundred men in there, of whom about two hundred and eighty had nothing to do with the film. In fact, I didn't recognise any of them! There was a guy squashed to my right with a peaked cap on, and I said to him, 'What's going on?'

'Naked girls, mate.'

'Ah, yes. And you are?'

'Terry. I drive the Tonibel ice-cream van. It's parked right outside. I'll do you a free cornet if you like when this is over.'

'Thanks! Who else is here?'

'Well, there's Geoff, he's the car park manager; that's Smithy over there, he does the wagons, and you probably know Slim Jim, the sandwich bloke. And that bloke over there's the one who's been selling the tickets. I think he's something to do with the church by the main entrance.'

I pushed my way to the side of the set and found someone from the crew. They looked worried. 'Ken'll go ballistic,' was all he said, and sure enough, the prophecy proved correct.

Ken walked in and his face was like thunder.

'Right, unless your name is one I am about to read out, then you have just thirty seconds to get out!' There were a few moans and groans because some of the guys had paid good money to see these twelve naked girls prance around this mountain, but Ken was having none of it.

For obvious reasons I can't allow his exact words to be printed in this book, but roughly translated he asked them all to go away in short jerky movements. And sure enough, within about half a minute the place was emptied.

A few days later I was in for the six o'clock meeting and Ken said, 'I've written a new part for the film. Wagner is going to have an alter ego in the form of Frankenstein.'

'Okay,' I say, thinking, *Why not? Of course!*

'He's in his laboratory and he's going to create the god Thor who he intends to set loose and conquer the world, but the experiment fails and Thor fails to come to life.'

'Great. So you want some music for this section of the film then?'

'Not exactly. Now tell me what you know about Thor, Rick,' said Ken.

'Not much,' I replied, 'although I think he was some sort of ancient god to the Germanic peoples.'

'And what's he look like?'

'No idea,' I answered.

'Well, take a look at this American comic, look at Thor and describe him to me.'

I took the glossy comic from him and studied Thor on the front cover.

'He's tall,' I started, 'long blond hair and . . . oh.' I looked across at Ken who was smiling.

'You've guessed it, Rick. You're Thor. You'll also note he's silver.'
'But I'm not silver, Ken,' I interjected.
'You will be soon. You're being sprayed in ten minutes.'

Half an hour later I was on the phone to my mum.
'You'll never guess what, Mum. I'm going to be in the film!'
'Really, Richard! How wonderful. Wait till I tell your father.'
'It's not a speaking part, but I will be on screen for about two minutes as the god Thor. I haven't actually got to move, I'll just be lying on this slab very still.'

The fact that all I was doing was lying still was irrelevant – she was delighted. Now, on occasions such as this I know for a fact that Mum went straight over to Chatterton's the greengrocer (which was in a little parade of shops where all the mums used to meet right opposite our house in Wood End Gardens in Northolt Park, a suburb of London in the county of Middlesex), ostensibly to buy half a pound of spam or some cheese but actually to tell the local gossips all the news. They'd have a shopping list of three items but be in there for two hours. Even as I put the phone down after making the call from the film set, I could see my mum putting her coat on and opening the door to rush over to Chatterton's. I could almost hear her saying, 'Yes, well, my Richard's in the movies now . . .'

Back at Shepperton, I went up to Costume and they started spraying me. Thankfully, this was someone who'd watched *Goldfinger*: they left my genitals unsprayed so I didn't suffocate. Then they glued these little diamantés in my eyebrows and stuck other spangly bits to me in various places. When I arrived on set, there were just Paul Nicholas as Wagner/Frankenstein, Roger Daltrey as Liszt and me as Thor.

'Right, this is what I want you to do, Rick,' said Ken. 'You lie on the slab and you don't move.' That was it. Wagner said something to Liszt about ruling the world and then that was that. End of scene.

I got up and felt really pleased with myself – although the fun was diluted a little by the painful two-hour scalding-hot shower and the petroleum-based industrial make-up remover that I had to use to scrape off all the silver spray. But still, I was delighted. *I was in the movies.*

Next morning Ken came into the six o'clock meeting.

'Rick, we've had a look at some of the rushes from the shoot and we don't think it's really working.'

Oh, what a shame, I thought. *But never mind, I tried my best.*

'So what we want to do is reshoot it. If you are supposed to be the god of the world, then you really ought to at least move. I think you've got to sit up. We're reshooting later this morning. Off you go. It's spray time again.'

Within two minutes of leaving Ken's office I was on the pay phone to my mum.

'Mum, guess what, I'm not just lying there any more – I've got to sit up!'

'Oh, Richard . . .'

She didn't care that I was only sitting up: this was as good as her boy being in an action blockbuster.

Coat goes on, door opens, over to Chatterton's.

The spray went on and yet more diamantés were stuck to the skin that had only really just calmed down from the two-hour scrubbing it'd had the day before.

I walked on to the set, trying my very best to act and look like a contemporary of Charlton Heston but in reality, probably looked more like a steward at Charlton Athletic. I laid on the slab and waited to be directed by Ken.

'Right, Rick, when Wagner says "I have created Thor who is going to conquer the world", you sit upright and just look straight ahead. Okay?' So I did this and we had to shoot a couple of takes but Ken was really pleased and sent me on my way back up to Costume for another two hours of agonising scrubbing and picking diamantés off my forehead.

Next morning I met Ken for our regular six o'clock meeting in the production office: 'Rick, I've looked at the rushes and it still doesn't work. It seems pretty obvious that when you sit up you should say something. So I'm going to write some words for you. Wagner will go on about how he created the god Thor, then Liszt will say something like, "Don't be so daft", at which point, Rick, you will sit upright and say the word "Stein", as in German for glass. It's also a very common part of a German surname and Wagner will look at you and say "Einstein?" and you will shake your head and simply say "Stein" again. Wagner will then look at you again and say "Bechstein?" and again you will shake your head and say "Nein . . . Bierstein!" Wagner will then hand you a large stein of lager, which you will drink. I know from your well-documented exploits that that part will be easy enough for you and you can be as messy as you like swilling it down. Being sprayed silver in ten minutes. Off you go.'

The phone rang at my mum's house.

'Mum, you know I had a moving part? Well, now I've got a speaking part as well!'

'Oh my word, Richard . . .'

As far as Mum was concerned, I was now one of the major stars of the film: I had reams of dialogue and pretty much the entire movie hung around my glorious acting talent.

Coat on, door open, over to Chatterton's.

This time, having learned my lesson, after we'd finished shooting I didn't scrub myself raw and spend all afternoon picking at my skin. I had a normal shower and got some of the silver off, but it was still very blotchy, especially around my face where the repeated sticking of diamantés had started to make my skin very red and puffy. I jumped in the car and headed home, but stopped off at a pub for a quick pint. I thought the locals were looking at me a little oddly but I ignored that, finished my pint and then went to the toilet before I carried on home.

While I was standing there, relieving myself of a couple of pints of best bitter, this middle-aged man came in to the toilet and took up his position in the adjacent urinal. He was ever so smiley. Rather too smiley for my liking.

'Hello,' he said, his eyes rather sparkly.

'All right, mate,' I replied.

'I haven't seen you in here before . . .'

I finished what I'd gone in there to do and walked over to the sink to wash my hands.

Smiley walked to the next sink and smiled at me again.

I looked up in the mirror and realised very quickly that I still had a lot of the silver make-up on my face and most of the diamantés in my eyebrows were still there. Sparkling too. I looked slightly to my left in the mirror and looked at Smiley. His make-up was slightly more pink and I recall he had more diamantés than me stuck everywhere.

'I know a nice little club . . .' he said.

'Sorry . . . really busy tonight,' I said.

'Never mind. Another time perhaps.'

This was 1975, remember. I later found out it was a well-known gay pub, which was blatantly obvious as I drove away and saw Smiley and a few of his mates clearly visible in my rear-view mirror, waving me off.

Next morning at six o'clock in the production office:

'Rick, it still doesn't work. I've looked at the rushes numerous times now and it just isn't happening. It seems pretty obvious that once you have drunk the beer you are supposed to go off and conquer the world as Wagner has told Listz he will. So I want you to go through everything again that we have done, but after all the beer drinking bit, get off the slab in quite a robotic fashion, walk to the French window which you will push open and then you will walk out and go off to conquer the world. You'll never be seen again. Spray time. Off you go.'

'Hello. Byron 6428.'

Even though telephones all had numbers now, Mum still answered as if it were the late 1950s.

'Mum, you know I had a moving part, and then a speaking part? Well, guess what? I've now got a walking part!'

'Oh my word, Richard . . .'

Mum's thinking Oscars, acclaim, red carpets . . .

Coat on, door open, over to Chatterton's.

Next morning at six o'clock in the production office: 'Rick, it *almost*, very nearly works, but not quite. It seems pretty obvious that, when you have drunk the beer, got off the table in quite a robotic fashion and walked to the French window, then it needs something more. Now, on your way to the French window, there's a fireplace with a log fire burning away beautifully that you have to pass. I want you to stop and pause by the fireplace, turn towards the flames and then put the fire out, before turning away and walking out to conquer the world.'

'And how do you want me to put the fire out, Ken?'

'Piss on it, Rick.'

'What?'

'You take your old chap out, piss on the fire, then put your old chap away, walk to the French window and go off to conquer the world. We're a bit strapped for time so get sprayed as quick as you can. On the set in an hour please.'

I didn't call Mum until the evening.

'Mum, this film, it's a really, *really* small part now – you won't even notice I'm in it. It certainly isn't worth going to see, honestly, please take my word for it. I wouldn't waste your time going, really I wouldn't. Go to a whist drive instead.'

'Don't be silly Richard? Don't go? You must be joking! You're starring in a major Ken Russell film and you've done the music. This is something I'll never forget!'

And she didn't.

And nor did the entire Wood End Residents' Association who Mum took with her.

I was told by my father that it was quite a long time before Mum went back across the road to shop at Chatterton's.

To her dying day, the film was never mentioned again.

NOT MY TIME

Some of you may know that my medical history is not exactly 'normal'. Having three heart attacks (albeit minor ones) at the age of twenty-five is but a blip on a lifetime of major scares and severe incidents. Of course, when you are in a rock band and in your mid-twenties, drinking every day to unbelievable excess and totally living the lifestyle, you are convinced that you're indestructible. Death isn't in the vocabulary. That happens to 'old people'. When you get a little older, however, you soon begin to realise that you are not immortal, which is a personal disaster for me as I know damn well that I won't get everything done that I want to in whatever time the good Lord has allotted me down here on Earth.

Jimmy Perry, who wrote *Dad's Army* along with David Croft, regularly hassled me to go and have a PSI blood test for prostate cancer from the age of fifty. I have since done this every year, religiously. I have lost more friends that I would care to mention from this killer. I've also got numerous friends whose lives have been saved by having this simple test annually and subsequently, with the cancer being caught early, have had the necessary treatment and are living full and active lives again.

The last time I went for my PSI blood test it turned out to be a little more complicated than the previous ones. As usual the doctor (who I know well), took my blood pressure, which they have to do before taking blood, looked up at me and said. 'Rick, would you mind just going for a walk round the park for half an hour or so? Then kindly come back.'

I presumed he had another patient to see urgently and so off I trotted for a nice walk around the park by the mere and wandered back to the surgery. He then took my blood pressure again, which I thought was a bit strange. He sat down opposite me and said, 'You've never ever had high blood pressure before have you?'

'No,' I replied. 'Always been on the button.'

'Well, you've got it now. I sent you for a walk hoping it might calm things down a bit, and it has, so I can take a blood test now.'

He blamed weight and stress and so I've been eating carefully ever since. Well, trying to eat less anyway! The problem is I love my food. I rarely if ever eat any fast food. I don't like burgers unless they're freshly made and cooked on a barbecue. I have the occasional pizza and once a month go to our favourite fish and chip restaurant, but the rest of the time it's healthy food and veg for the Wakemans. I have quite a sizeable vegetable plot which I actually do myself! (That's shocked you, I know, but that's what happens to ageing rockers when they reach sixty. They go for lovely walks on the beach or the fens, grow vegetables, mow the lawn, get up three times for a wee during the night . . . yes, your rock 'n' roll years are certainly behind you when you hit late middle age, that's for sure.) Now, my much better half, Rachel, is a jour-nalist and writes regularly for different health columns in the newspapers. Back when we first got together, she said I needed to have a proper medical (I think she was seeing if I'd live or not). She suggested I went and had a thorough BUPA check.

I told her I'd already had one about eight years ago and she asked how it went. I explained to her that I probably wasn't as well prepared for the examination as I should have been. You see, they are very, *very* thorough. They sent me tons of literature to read and a video to look at (it's a DVD these days). You get this pile of stuff through the post but, like most people, I thought, *Nah, I haven't got time to look at all this.* I put it somewhere and never found it again. *Come on, what are they gonna do that I should have to read up about? A few blood samples? No problem.*

For this particular examination, they have got you all day – it's a really lengthy medical and very thorough. I went to the then BUPA hospital in Warrington and checked in. I have to say, they make you feel very at ease from the moment you walked in. The break for lunch is somewhat uninspiring as you get to eat lettuce leaves and if you're lucky a slice of cucumber. I'd given them some samples that they'd said I needed to bring (they'd told me this in the accompanying letter that came with all the stuff that I'd lost) and I was feeling pretty jovial, laughing and joking with the nurses. I got on an exercise bike and they ran some heart tests – given my history that was always going to raise a few eyebrows – and everything was going great.

I went off for lunch and tried to get excited about my lettuce leaf. A load more tests continued after lunch and I was wired up to different machines. Lungs were checked, everything really. I was very impressed I have to say.

At 4 p.m. precisely (I know the time exactly, because what happened next remains indelibly emblazoned on my mind and still sends the odd shiver up my back) I was asked to go to another examination room and lie down on my side. The doctor walked in and started prodding my back and stomach and generally giving me another once-over. As he did so, he was saying, 'Did you get all the literature we sent about what today was all about, Rick?'

'Yes, oh yes, thank you, really interesting.'

'And the video, Rick?'

'Oh, yes, really helpful, eye-opening in fact,' I said.

. . . and it was as if this last statement of mine suddenly became a prophecy . . .

'Stay on your side and just lower your underpants for me please and tuck your knees up a little . . . that's right.'

I started to feel a little apprehensive. Why was I being placed in this unusual position? I said to myself.

It was the sound of the Marigold gloves going on that was the giveaway I suppose.

The doctor spoke.

'As you have watched the videos and read all the literature sent to you, Rick, then you'll no doubt be expecting this . . .' (with an emphasis on the 'this').

Needless to say, I wasn't.

I couldn't make a noise while he appeared to be exploring my interior inch by inch. After about a minute of him rummaging around, I mustered up enough composure to say, 'I think you'll find that my tonsils are fine, doctor.'

He finished his examination, removed himself from my posterior and, as he thanked me and walked out of the room, said, 'You *didn't* watch the video, did you?'

'Er, no. How did you know?'

'Because the men who do know exactly what to expect during the medical and are always a little nervous until the internal examination is over. You have been much too jovial!'

'Can I ask you a question please, doctor?'

'Of course, Rick. Fire away.'

By now, I admit to being extremely nervous.

'Is there anything else I should have looked at and may regret not doing so?'

Another unrelated inspection of the nether regions also caught me out. After my personal experience with medical interference of my genital region, I would not advise any man of a sane and sensible mind to have a vasectomy. It is not what people think.

There is more than one type of 'snip'. Yes, there is the 'little snip', a fifteen-minute job while you're discussing football as the doctor fiddles around down below. But that's not a hundred per cent fail-safe. It has been known for a few of the little soldiers to lurk in some internal sperm shelter that protects Sergeant Tadpole and the rest of the platoon, and once the coast is clear, out they come to do their bidding.

So what I'm talking about is the guaranteed, no more live soldiers, all over, genitally dead for ever, blank firing, full-on, general-anaesthetic, non-reversible Full Monty.

It is *agony*.

Guess which one I had?

I went into the hospital on the Isle of Man. This was the first operation I'd ever had in my life so I knew nothing about what was going to happen. My good friend and next-door neighbour Bill Collister drove me there. I said I would drive myself, but he said he knew of somebody who'd had the full on 'no more babies' operation and he wasn't really able to drive afterwards. During the trip to the hospital I asked Bill how long it was before his mate could drive again and Bill said, 'Oh, three or four.'

'Hours? Well, that's not too bad.'

'Days.'

I was already having second thoughts but it was too late. We were at the hospital and I was being checked in.

It was nine o'clock in the morning and I was lying in the bed when this quite pretty nurse came into the private room with a shaving bowl full of foam and a shaving brush and razor.

'Can you shave, please, Mr Wakeman?'

As I mentioned earlier, I'd never had an operation before, so knew nothing about the procedures.

Shave?

Why? My chin was nowhere near my testicles.

I smiled sweetly back at her.

'Is it absolutely necessary? I've had this beard for about thirty years.'

She explained my mistake and said, 'Sister will be back in thirty minutes to check that your pubic area is suitably prepared.'

Prepared for what? The hairdresser?

I gently lifted back the sheet and looked down at 'willy'. I'm sure he looked back up at me. I'm not sure who was the most terrified, him or me.

I started shaving myself but I was making a right dog's dinner of it. This was the moment I discovered that 'willy' is actually telepathic. As I was shaving, I could hear his little voice inside my head, calling me, pleading with me. 'I'll never forgive you for this,' he said.

I did the best I could, but I made a terrible job of it. We are not talking as smooth as a baby's bum; in fact, it was more like Velcro by the time I'd finished. I know this for a fact because when I stood up the towel stuck to me!

Then the door burst open and in came a woman who I suppose in days gone by would have been called Matron. I personally would have called her Hippopotamus.

My first thought was that she was probably the love-child of Hattie Jaques and Brian Blessed. She whipped my towel away and tutted. She said, 'That won't do, Mr Wakeman, not at all.' Then, to my stunned amazement, she got hold of the razor, grabbed hold of 'willy' and shaved away every single tiny wisp of hair that was visible to the naked eye.

'Willy' spoke to me again.

'You will pay for this, Wakeman. You will pay for this within an inch of your life. This is just not acceptable. Boy, will you regret this.'

'Sorry.' I said.

'And so you should be,' said Matron Hippo.

'I wasn't talking to you,' I said.

'Well, who were you talking to then?' she asked.

'Willy.'

'Silly man,' she muttered and left the room.

126

I was wheeled in for the operation and felt the world was against me. The nurse was against me, Matron Hippo was against me, the surgeon was probably against me and 'willy' absolutely hated me. *Would our relationship ever be the same?* I asked myself as I slowly succumbed to the anaesthetic.

When I came round, I remember thinking, Why are my testicles on fire?

It was three days before I felt comfortable walking at all. Four days before sitting down and standing up wasn't unbearable, six days before I was able to drive, eight days before I could comfortably take a golf ball out of the hole and three and a half months before 'Willy' spoke to me again.

So, whenever I hear a man say he is going for a vasectomy, I sit him down gently and counsel him and invariably he changes his mind.

Although I have to watch what I eat sometimes, and I am aware of the risks and the foods I need to avoid, I have to say I am probably healthier at the time of writing than I ever have been. However, this has not always been the case. When I was doing *Return to the Centre of the Earth*, I was working a minimum of twenty hours a day, sometimes actually doing fifty- and sixty-hour shifts. Totally stupid, but I had no choice. Deadlines loomed and they had to be met. This kind of lifestyle has to catch up on you at some point.

It did. And when it did, it almost cost me my life.

Unbeknown to me, the abyss was just around the corner when I flew out to Los Angeles to meet and work with Patrick Stewart. I'd already got quite a few guests involved already, people like Bonnie Tyler, Justin Hayward and Ozzy Osborne. Now I had to travel to America to record Patrick Stewart for the narration. I already felt ill on the flight going over and was constantly short of breath. By the time I got to the hotel in Beverly Hills I was finding it really hard to breathe. I felt I was actually inhaling and exhaling okay, but it didn't seem like anything was happening or that any oxygen was going in. I felt disorientated, dizzy and had a strange tingling sensation.

Undeterred, I headed to the studio to record Patrick's wonderful voice. He was a lovely, lovely man. We'd rented a particular studio that he personally liked using. He was due at ten o'clock to start recording and I had him from ten until three, so there was a lot to get through. I arrived at about nine and there were already quite a few people there – his 'pre-entourage' had arrived. You've got to remember that Patrick is a huge Hollywood star. People were running around going, 'Have we got his 10.45 bagel? Is it seeded? And his coffee? The one he likes? . . . and who are you?' One of them actually spoke to me!

'I'm Rick Wakeman. Patrick's doing the narration for me.'

'Oh yes. Well, he'll be here in a minute, He was picked up at 9.15. He'll have a coffee, possibly something light to eat, and then recording can start. Breaks will be at 11 a.m., 12 p.m. or whenever Patrick sees fit. We'll be on hand all the time for any other needs.'

Oh my God, this is going to be a nightmare.

I'd never met him before so it was with some trepidation that I shook his hand when he arrived – bang on time. Completely in contrast to what I'd expected from his panic-stricken entourage, Patrick was just so charming, he was delightful. One of the first things he said to me was, 'Rick, I read the story and all the narration. It's a great yarn and I love a good yarn. Do you want me to read exactly as you've written it or are you open to a few suggestions?'

Naturally I welcomed any suggestions from a man as talented as Patrick, and we tweaked a little here and there and really enjoyed working together. Then at 10.45, a lady walked in and said, 'Patrick, it's 10.45, time for your bagel.'

Very calmly and in that sublime voice, he said, 'I don't want a bagel, thank you.'

'But it's 10.45, you said—'

'I don't want a bagel, thank you. We're busy. Lots to get through.'

The lady left the room muttering quite audibly, 'But he always has a bagel at 10.45.'

Patrick turned to me and said, 'Welcome to Hollywood, Rick. You get the entourage wherever you go. They're lovely people and really care about everything and want to do the best for you to keep you happy and so on, but the truth is, sometimes they can drive you nuts. But it's the way things are.'

Patrick was reading beautifully but because of the considerable changes we'd made, we started to run behind schedule. His work rate was brilliant, it was only because of the changes, he was really working hard at it. He really did care about the narrative. I only had him till three and by one o'clock I was only about 30 per cent done.

At 2.45, another lady (not the bagel lady) walked in and said, 'Patrick, we have to leave in exactly fifteen minutes.'

'I'm not ready, though. I haven't finished,' he replied, again very politely.

'But you have another appointment, Mr Stewart.'

'Not any more.'

'It's very important, Mr Stewart.'

'Could you move it for me please. Thank you.'

Patrick was never anything but gentle and polite, no matter how frustrated he was. After that, he carried on working until 8 p.m. and finished the entire narration before finally heading home. By the time I left down the studio and got back to my own hotel, I was feeling very positive about the project: the day with Patrick had been a real joy. I would love to work with him again. He has everything. Superb acting ability and the voice to go with it!

Physically, however, I was feeling *dreadful*.

Early the following day I drove up into the Hollywood Hills to meet with Trevor Rabin, the phenomenally talented guitarist formerly of Yes and now a very successful composer of film music in his own right. Trev and I had become great friends on the Yes Union tour and he very kindly said he'd love to be part of the *Return to the Centre of the Earth* album and so I wrote a song especially for him entitled 'Never is a Long Long Time'.

By the time I drove back to the hotel later that evening I felt dreadful. The jet lag had kicked in earlier in the week but this was something different. I slept badly then got up early to fly back to the UK. I think in retrospect I shouldn't have got on the plane home at all. I was really struggling for breath, I felt faint, I was really unwell.

The entire journey back to the Isle of Man was a bit of a blur, but I struggled home and fell into bed at about ten o'clock on Friday night. I was due to start work again at 6 a.m. at my office in Peel, writing more orchestrations but I just couldn't face it – I thought I'd go nuts if I didn't have a break. So I got the old golf clubs out and went for a morning round at Peel Golf Club. (Don't worry, I'll come to my golf career later.) I thought that would set me up for the rest of the day – fresh air, relaxation. I put my feeling so rough down to overwork and tiredness and that some outdoor exercise would do me the power of good.

However, after only about three holes I was fighting for breath and I had to abandon the game. My playing partners were very concerned and said I looked really ill and shouldn't drive, but I assured them I was okay and loaded up the car with my golf stuff and started to drive the six miles home. In the car, I started to get these violent stabbing pains in my head, and the journey back took me over half an hour – I was crawling along. I felt like someone was hammering sharp nails into my brain, I'd never felt anything like it in my life.

I went straight to bed but as I lay there I couldn't breathe. Out of all the things I've been through in my life – all the scrapes, health scares, illnesses, everything – not being able to breathe has been the most frightening. I was opening my mouth but nothing was happening. And I was still getting all this violent stabbing pain in my head. I was involuntarily thrashing around on the bed. I was in total agony. Within half an hour the doctor arrived. She didn't spend very long examining me. She didn't have to, and an ambulance was sent for. I lost consciousness as they carried me across the driveway to the ambulance.

I didn't know it at the time, but I was in *big* trouble.

What followed was a very peculiar experience. I hit semi-consciousness as they wheeled me into the hospital. However, I had no energy at all: I couldn't move so although I was vaguely aware of what was going on I didn't have any strength to say or do anything. I was like a silent witness to my own emergency – it was really strange.

I was aware that they were sticking things in my arm. I was also aware of a drip being inserted and quite a lot of medical staff bustling around me. Then I seemed to recall something being stuck in my lower back, it was very painful, but I didn't have the strength to cry out.

I was then put into a sort of plastic cocoon which I can only presume was an oxygen tent. A mask was also over my face – I am guessing it was to assist with my breathing – and then I drifted off into a very calm and soothing state of deep sleep, a form of induced coma, I suppose.

Next thing I recall is hearing two voices. I didn't really know where I was but I could hear two voices. They were speaking softly and slightly anxiously. As I listened, I noticed that I felt very, very light, as if I weighed nothing. I tried to focus in on the words being said.

'The next forty-eight hours are critical. With the double pneumonia and pleurisy he needs the antibiotics to kick in very soon and start working or else he won't make it. We need to inform the family.'

I couldn't move. I wanted to, but I couldn't even open my eyes to see or mouth to talk. It was just like a nightmare where it's all so real but you can't move or do anything to change what is happening.

However, my thought patterns were extremely clear. I knew I was seriously ill. I knew I was in hospital. I was also acutely aware of everything that was going on around me. I can remember very clearly thinking to myself: *This can't be right*. I do have a strong Christian belief and faith, but I will also temper that with the fact that I have never taken drugs in my life and at this stage I hadn't had any alcohol for years. So what happened next was not hallucinatory.

I remember that through my thoughts I spoke very clearly to God.

I said to him: *God, you've screwed up really badly here. You gave me the talent and the means to write and record* Return to the Centre of the Earth, *and I've not finished it. There's loads still to do.*

It really was that specific.

Nobody else knows how it all fits together. If I die, it won't ever be finished, or if it is, it won't be right, so you've cocked up somewhere. Please check again. I can't possibly be due to die now, please look again. You really must have got it wrong.

After that I don't remember anything else.

The next thing I recall, I was coming round in a different hospital bed with an oxygen mask over my face. A nurse came into the room and said, 'Hello. Awake are we? Would you like something to drink?' Then the doctor came in and asked me how I was feeling. I ached and felt really tired. I started coughing up all sorts of gunge and the nurse gave me a bowl to spit it into. 'As much as you can bring up,' she said.

'What day is it?' I asked.

'Wednesday afternoon – you've been out since Saturday . You are still quite seriously ill, Rick. You're not out of the woods yet. You have double pneumonia and pleurisy.'

'I know,' I said and she looked at me somewhat puzzled wondering how on earth I could know.

'It could be worse. At one stage we thought you had legionnaires' disease but we checked for that and you're all right.'

I suppose the realisation that I was very ill only sank in an hour later when in walked all my kids. Oliver and Adam had been flown in from England and Ben from Switzerland to join Oscar and Jemma who lived on the Isle of Man. They looked very very worried.

'Don't worry,' I said. 'I'm not that ill.'

'You are,' said Oliver.

'Oh,' I said.

Over the next few days, the physio would come to see me, wrap a towel round his fist and punch me in order to bring up more stuff in my lungs through the pleurisy. This was exhausting, but I was glad to be awake and aware of all that was going on.

I later found out that they often induced a coma to combat pneumonia. I'm led to understand that they did this with my great friend Jeremy Beadle, but sadly he didn't recover, which I'm told can happen.

To cut a long story short, I was in hospital for quite some time. One lung had been totally full of gunge with the pleurisy and pneumonia and the other had pretty much collapsed and so it was no wonder that I couldn't breathe. They said that I had made one lifestyle choice that was my saving grace: 'If you were a smoker, Rick, you'd be dead.' I recalled the day in October 1979 when I smoked my last cigarette and thanked the good Lord for bringing me to my senses.

I lost a phenomenal amount of weight whilst in hospital and when I finally got home it kept dropping off as well (the weight that is, I haven't returned to the vasectomy story!). In the space of four months I went from seventeen stone to eleven stone. Sadly, these days I'm back up to seventeen stone again!

* * *

One last piece to add to this story. Just before being discharged from Nobles Hospital on the Isle of Man, where I have to say I was wonderfully cared for throughout my stay, I asked the doctor to come and see me.

'Can I ask you something?' I said to him. 'I know I was completely out of it for several days, but whilst in this comatose state, I can distinctly recall hearing voices,' and I told him the conversation I thought I'd heard.

'Rick, that conversation did take place. I was one of those two people you heard. But we were not in your room. We were standing outside quite a way away.'

'Wow. So how can you explain that?'

'Well, it's not a total surprise, Rick. You were *very* ill. It is quite widely accepted in the medical profession that as you begin to die your senses start to shut down but your hearing is actually heightened and is most probably the last sense to go. It's one of the body's last acts before death. We believe that people in comas or deep states of unconsciousness have a much-heightened sense of hearing too. Someone up there likes you, Rick.'

'Can't be sure about that,' I said, 'but I did send Him a message.'

CARS

I've always loved cars. It's my only fetish nowadays: I don't smoke, I don't drink, I've never been a clubber, I don't go on fantastic first-class holidays around the world. I don't live a flash lifestyle, so cars are among the few passions I've always been happy to indulge in. (How I came to buy my first car is in the first book in this series; apparently iTunes sell it on audio.)

Back in 1972 I was living in Gerrards Cross and I drove a beautiful left-hand drive convertible Mk 1 red E-type Jag. Totally impractical but it was a beauty. Loads of rock 'n' rollers and foot-ballers were driving them. I was on the phone to my dad one day – although he wasn't a great car fanatic in any way we'd always gone to the Motor Show every year together throughout the 1950s and 1960s (Those were the days. Rows and rows of high quality British made cars. I stopped going in the 1980s. Too depressing). So I always kept him up to date as to what my latest four-wheeled acquisition was. The Jag had replaced a Ford Zephyr Six. I was telling him all about it and he said, 'What are you going to do when you want to take your dogs out to the country for a long walk?'

'Good point, Dad,' I agreed. 'I need another car for that!' Any excuse, really. So I decided that this was going to be a 'car day' and I found the telephone number for a Volvo dealership in Reading. I rang them up and said, 'Have you got any Volvo estates?'

'Just the one. It's blue,' said the salesman on the other end of the phone.

'That'll do,' I said and bought the car. It was a very safe buy as it had a full parts and labour warranty and anyway Volvos had a reputation for not going wrong as well as being thoroughly reliable. They were also thoroughly boring, but you could get loads in them, including two dogs!

Two days later it was on my driveway. I had that car for a long time; it really was boring but it was bloody useful.

With the Volvo being so practical, I started to use the E-type a lot less and it was also playing up a little bit. So I began to look around for a replacement, in other words another car that I wouldn't use much but was at least in working order and a bit different. I phoned up David Moss, my accountant and asked him how much I could spend on another car. 'No more than two grand, Rick please,' came his response. A nice smile crept across my face. You could buy a very decent car for £2,000 back in 1973.

I fancied a nice XJ6 so I bought a copy of *Exchange & Mart* (*Auto Trader* hadn't started by then). I've always loved looking at magazines like that. I still get *Auto Trader* every week just to look through. It's like petrol-head pornography. Anyway, as I was flicking through the pages of the jolly old *Exchange & Mart*, my eyes caught a small advert which said, 'Rolls-Royces from £2,000'. Now my dad had always said to me, 'Son, the car to aspire to is a Rolls-Royce. Best car in the world.' So, with my dad's words ringing in my ears, I dialled the number in the advertisement.

The man who answered the phone was a private car dealer by the name of Dickie Hicks and he ran his business from his house in Hampstead.

'Hello, yes, I saw your advert in *Exchange & Mart* for Rolls-Royces from two thousand pounds,' I stated.

'Yes, that's right,' he replied.

'Well, what have you got?'

'Rolls-Royces from two thousand pounds. That's why I put the advert in.'

I drove to the address, which turned out to be a very nice big house in the very poshest part of Hampstead. I knocked on the door and it was answered by Dickie Hicks himself.

'Come in!'

He was sitting behind a desk in the hallway of his home. He looked me up and down – remember, I had hair hanging way down my back and usually looked pretty dishevelled.

'What do you want?' he said, a little abruptly.

'I called you earlier about the Rolls-Royce . . .'

'How much have you got?' he asked.

'Two thousand pounds,' I said.

He nodded and beckoned for me to go with him. We got in his car and drove for about two miles to a petrol station that had an enormous warehouse to one side, almost like an aircraft hangar. He pushed open the heavy doors and when I saw what was in there my eyes nearly popped out. Inside, nose to nose, bumper to bumper, were line after line of Rolls-Royces. They were mainly Silver Cloud 1s, 2s and 3s. I stood there, gob-smacked at what I was seeing. A real-life Aladdin's Cave of Rolls-Royces. I could have just stood amongst them all day.

'Two thousand pounds, you said,' mused Dickie.

'That's right,' I said.

We almost literally waded our way through all these wonderful cars and eventually he opened the door on a Cloud 1. I looked inside and it was all leather and wood, quite stunning. Everything you'd expect a Rolls-Royce to be. Dicky put a key in the ignition and tried to start the engine, but the battery was completely flat, so he went and got a mechanic to jump-start it. As the engine turned over and kicked into life a huge plume of thick smoke spat out of the shaking exhaust. Not ideal.

'Don't worry about that, we can have that fixed,' Dicky said, rather unconvincingly.

I began to look over the car and noticed the paintwork was far from pristine. In fact, much of the rear half was covered in small rust bubbles. I was peering down looking at these when Dickie said, 'Don't worry about that, we can have that fixed too. You can have this one for two grand, just give us a couple of days to fix the exhaust.'

I admit to not being totally convinced, but I'd come out to buy a Rolls-Royce, and a Rolls-Royce I was going to buy.

I suddenly became aware of Dickie studying me a little more closely than before.

'What do you do for a living, anyway?' He was perhaps understandably curious about someone who looked like me asking after a Rolls-Royce.

'I'm a rock 'n' roll musician,' I explained.

'Oh, right. People don't normally associate rock 'n' roll musicians with Rolls-Royces. Any of the other guys in your band got a Rolls-Royce?'

'No, but when everyone sees this I think that might change! I reckon it could start a bit of a trend.'

'Really? Would you point them in my direction if they liked yours?'

'Yeah, sure.'

'Right, well, in that case, don't buy that one – it's a piece of shit,' he said and walked off towards a much shinier, nicer condition Roller.

'This is what you want, not that piece of crap. This is actually two thousand, seven hundred and fifty pounds but you can have it for two grand if you pass the word on.'

We did the deal and I did indeed 'pass the word on'. In fact, over the next few years, I put Dickie in touch with quite a few rock 'n' rollers who bought cars from him, and indeed within two years I was dealing myself, in partnership with another dealer called Peter Vernon-Kell. We sold cars to the likes of Roger Daltrey, John Entwistle, Jon Anderson, Alan White, Chris Squire and even 'Deal-a-Day' Lane. All in all, over a period of about four years, I reckon I supplied more than forty cars to the rock 'n' roll industry!

At one stage I had twenty-two cars. The collection included Clark Gable's 1957 Cadillac Limousine. I had a beautiful MG TD, six Rolls-Royce Cloud 1s, and four Silver Shadows. I also had a couple of Jags, a Phantom 2 (actually owned by Henry Royce himself at one time), two Phantom 3s, and a Mk 6 Bentley, to name but a few.

It often got printed in the music press that I had this collection of cars. The truth was I had a car company: we *rented* cars out. We had chauffeurs on our books and they were hired out for weddings and special events and occasionally to bands who wanted to travel around on tour a little more luxuriously and somewhat differently.

It was called The Fragile Carriage Company and I always told the journalists about this, but somehow that never made it into the feature, it was always left as 'Prog Rock Star Has 22 Cars'. To be fair, I guess I can see why that made better reading.

Sadly, I sold my last Bentley about three years ago. To be honest, having expensive cars has become more trouble than it's worth. I don't think it's unfair to say that when I was a kid, if someone had a nice car then all us schoolboys would stop and just look at it and be knocked out. Nowadays, in my experience, if you've got a nice car and you park it somewhere, then the odds are that when you come back someone will have gone down the side of it with a key, slashed the tyres, or ripped your wipers off. It's very hard to own a nice car that you can actually leave it safely anywhere. Why do people do that?

Mind you, cars are still my passion. I don't always think straight when I see a beautiful car. If I was ever really wealthy again – which is as about likely as the Pope giving birth – remember I've been divorced three times! – I would definitely buy another Rolls-Royce. A black one I think!

Given my passion for cars, one of the most disastrous situations to possibly find yourself in would be that of being banned from driving and to lose your licence . . . but that's exactly what once happened to me.

It was a disastrous combination of golf, a curry, a football match, a gold Rolls-Royce, and a large brandy washed down with a pint of lager that led to my downfall.

Back in the mid-1980s, my Saturdays were very special to me. I had a routine when I was not on tour that I stuck to rigidly. Firstly I would go to Foxhills golf club, where I was a member, and play with my usual friends in a four ball in whatever the competition was that day.

Then I would either have a spot of lunch in the clubhouse or drive into Camberley where I lived and have a spot of lunch at a very nice Italian bistro, before going off to watch Camberley Town lose. I was the chairman of Camberley Town, as you well know from an earlier chapter.

It was April, right at the end of the football season, a beautiful spring morning, so at 7 a.m. I set off for the golf club. I played a half-decent round and set off for Camberley to the Italian Bistro as the clubhouse restaurant was closed because of some private function that was taking place.

Unfortunately, the Italian place I usually went to was closed for refurbishment. I was starving, but didn't fancy pub grub so found myself in a less than salubrious curry house with a reputation that could at best be described as 'iffy'. However, it was the only place open and I was really hungry so I went in there anyway; for some reason known only to myself at the time I decided to have a vindaloo for lunch. Perhaps not my wisest decision. Even as I was eating this meal I could feel my stomach rumbling and protesting – you could almost hear it saying, 'Rick! No! Don't do this! This is not a good move!' But I was absolutely famished so I polished it all off and headed down to the football club, resplendent in my Camberley Town blazer emblazoned with the club badge.

The intestinal alarm bells were ringing all the way through the first half, fuelled, no doubt, by the brandy and beer I had sunk too. By half-time the bowel region was complaining noisily and with odour-producing regularity.

Now, to anyone who knows anything about semi-professional football clubs it's a simple fact that the toilet facilities are not exactly great – and dear old Camberley Town was no exception. So despite the thunderous noises from down below and the increasing stomach cramps, I was determined to avoid the some-what less than luxurious toiletry facilities (a cubicle with a door would have been nice), and hold on until I got home after the game.

Immediately after the final whistle blew I went into the committee room and congratulated the visiting chairman on his team's 7–1 victory. By now, my stomach was really starting to convulse. From the look on his face it was very apparent that both his hearing and sense of smell were in fine working order and that a certain area of my body was giving both these senses a thorough testing.

'Are you okay, Rick?' he asked me politely but with obvious concern.

'To be honest,' I replied, 'I had what appears to be an iffy curry at lunchtime and it's going through me like a Ferrari. I think this is going to be an "at home with the *Daily Telegraph* job". It's certainly not anything that the Camberley Town lavatorial pipe work is anywhere near prepared for.'

I think he was relieved to see me turn to leave the room. So were all the other committee members, if I'm honest. Maybe it was my imagination, but I'm sure I heard their chairman turn to Roy Calver and say with some concern, 'I'd alert the Thames Water Authority if I were you, Mr Vice Chairman.'

I exited the room rather rapidly and jumped into my gold Rolls-Royce Silver Shadow. I only lived a mile up the road so very soon I'd be home, sitting on my nice Armitage Shanks with the *Daily Telegraph*, but that was not to be. I drove out of Krooner Park and pulled out into the traffic and I can categorically state that I was doing exactly thirty-five mph, because I was in a line of cars and we were all doing the same speed.

Then I noticed a police motorcyclist with a radar gun standing on the corner of a side road. Pointing at me to pull over.

Great!

I knew all the local Old Bill but as I wound down the window I realised this one wasn't a local guy. However, he knew who I was.

'Mr Wakeman, have you just come from Camberley Town Football Club?'

'Yes, I have.'

'Have you had a drink down there, Mr Wakeman?'

'Yes, I've had a brandy and a beer.'

'Well, you've admitted the fact that you've had a drink so I'm going to give you an alcohol breath test.'

I got out of the car and blew into the electronic breathalyser.

'Mr Wakeman, you have failed the breathalyser test,' said the copper and then proceeded to read out my rights to me. I have to say I wasn't listening because I was concentrating so hard on not shitting myself, literally. He then said he would radio for a police car to come and take me to Camberley Police Station.

Which was less than half a mile away.

By now a few locals had gathered on their doorsteps to see what all the fuss was about.

Suddenly, horrifically, my stomach decided it didn't want to house the vindaloo anymore and made internal preparations to send it on its way. Breathalyser or not. I actually remember gritting my teeth to hold it in.

To nip it in the bud, so to speak.

I spoke to the policeman, who was obviously more concerned that a patrol car hadn't yet arrived to take me to the police station.

'Excuse me, officer,' I said very politely. 'I've got a *really* bad stomach due to a particularly dodgy curry that I had at lunchtime – I know you're waiting for a police car but the police station is only four hundred yards away, I'm quite happy to walk there because I am so desperate for the toilet.'

'You're not going anywhere. You'll do what I tell you and you'll stay here.'

'Well, can't I go into someone's house?' (By now there were more people watching this than there had been at the Camberley Town football match.)

'You'll do exactly as you're told and wait for the squad car.'

At this point, another police motorcyclist arrived at the scene and fortunately I knew this guy quite well. Let's call him Murray. I was so relieved.

'You don't look too well, Rick. Are you all right?'

'No, Murray, I'm not all right, I've just failed a breathalyser test and I'm in desperate need of the toilet. I went to the Indian for lunch you see . . .'

'I can guess which one. We're actually keeping an eye on that place. So are the health authorities.'

'Bit late for me.'

My cheeks were firmly clenched together but gas was still able to escape somehow.

'You're not well are you?' said Murray, his nose wrinkling at the change in air pressure.

At this point the miserable police motorcyclist who had nicked me piped up. 'I have arrested this gentleman for being DUI. Why have they sent a bike? I radio-ed for a car.'

'We haven't got a car available, so they sent me,' replied Officer Murray.

'Look, gents, this is all very interesting but as you can see for yourselves, I am smartly dressed in expensive clothes and at any moment I am likely to shit myself. Now, I am not prepared to do that and spoil my nice clothes. So if necessary I shall just drop my trousers and crap right here on the pavement.'

I continued my rhetoric with a genuine element of pleading. 'Please can I use somebody's toilet before this all starts to get very messy. Literally.'

By now, Murray was sniggering out loud while the miserable copper was becoming increasingly heated.

He didn't find it funny at all.

So he put me in an armlock.

All I was capable of doing at this precise point in time was to just about control myself from not having a very nasty accident, so I'm not sure why he thought I represented enough of a threat to use an armlock. With me twisted half over and about to explode any second, he frogmarched me across the road to confront this woman standing on her doorstep.

'Madam, do you have a downstairs toilet?'

'Yes, officer.'

'Then I am commandeering said toilet for the use of my prisoner.'

With me still in an armlock, he marched into her house, opened the downstairs toilet door and said to Murray, 'Watch him. Don't let him out of your sight,' and then he inspected the toilet. Probably for escape hatches, I suppose. Maybe he'd had a past experience of a criminal in his custody who'd tried to escape round the U-Bend. I don't know. Anyway he then shoved me in with a grunt.

By now I didn't care: I was in a toilet and about to relieve the volcano waiting to erupt. I went to shut the door and a big black policeman's boot stuck itself in the doorway so I couldn't close it.

'You're not shutting the door, son. Oh no!'

'You've got no idea what's coming, have you officer?' I said, now well beyond caring.

I pulled down my trousers and underpants and sat down and took stock of the ludicrous nature of my situation.

There I was, trousers down by my ankles, with my Camberley Town Blazer on, in a complete stranger's toilet after being arrested for drink-driving with an irate policeman's size fourteen boot in the door. I remember thinking to myself, *What on earth else could possibly happen on top of this ridiculous scenario? . . .* When at that precise moment, through a gap in the door came my *Journey to the Centre of the Earth* album cover accompanied by a woman's voice which said, 'Would you sign this for my son Geoffrey please?'

'He can't sign anything – he's under arrest,' said Constable-Boot-in-the-Door.

'He's using my toilet!' came her not unreasonable reply.

I signed the album.

The police tests revealed later that I'd registered just one unit over the legal limit of 80. Unfortunately, this was irrelevant: in terms of the law I might as well have been 200, either way. The irony was that this happened in the April of that year and by the following August I'd stopped drinking altogether. The case actually came up in the September so I was already teetotal by the time I went to court. I can't even get done for drink-driving normally.

I must admit that I was very concerned on the day of the court hearing at Camberley Magistrates Court because at that particular time the courts were often using celebrities as an example. They'd already sent George Best to prison, they were handing out massive fines and suspended sentences all over the place. My lawyer sat me down and said, 'Rick, there's bad news and possibly even worse news. The bad news is that you could get a suspended sentence for this, even for one point over the limit.

They've got the knives out for actors, footballers and musicians at the moment.'

'Crikey, if that's the bad news, what's the even worse news?'

'The even worse news is that if they really wanted to use you as a high-profile example, they might send you down, but if that's the case, call me and we'll sort out an appeal.'

I was really panicking. I walked down to the court as I knew full well it was pointless driving down there as I wouldn't be able to drive back.

My case was called and the three magistrates listened to the proceedings. I had no case to answer. It was cut and dried. The prosecuting policeman said his bit, and seemed thrilled that he'd nabbed someone with a bit of profile. The press were in attendance too and he was obviously playing to them. I was told a few months later that after my conviction he threw a party to celebrate.

Then the chief magistrate addressed me.

'Mr Wakeman, in some senses you were unlucky. You were only one point over the limit. However, this just illustrates that drinking and driving is a matter of black and white – the only way to be one hundred per cent certain of passing a breath test is to drink nothing. I'm going to ban you for a period of one year and issue you with a fine of one hundred and forty pounds . . .'

I have to be honest, I couldn't help breathing a fairly hefty sigh of relief.

I handed my licence to the duty sergeant in the court, who I knew well. He knew I'd been unlucky, but realised that it could have been a lot worse and told me so. 'Think back, Rick,' he said to me over the desk whilst completing the paperwork. 'When you were driving up that road, even if you hadn't been doing five miles over the limit, and a child had run out in front of you or peddled out on a bike and you had either injured or killed that child – even if it was not your fault and there were witnesses to confirm that – then it would all have become irrelevant once you had taken a breath test and failed. Then you would have been in very serious trouble and more than likely facing a lengthy custodial sentence. Simple facts would state that you killed or injured a child while driving under the influence of alcohol. So I'd like you to remember how lucky you are that you are not standing here facing that charge.'

What he said really hit home to me. I had stopped drinking altogether by then, but had I still been drinking his words would have had the desired effect and I have drummed into my kids and in fact many other people that it's just not worth having even one drink and then getting behind the wheel of a car.

A few weeks after the court case, my wedding was fast approaching as was the stag night at the Camberley Town Football Club. We wanted to get an extended licence but because CTFC was very close to Sandhurst and Aldershot – both extremely famous for their involvement with the army – the magistrates rarely agreed to extensions for any of the pubs or licenced premises, maybe half an hour if you were lucky; it was very difficult to have lock-ins because the police were very strict. Roy Calver offered to apply for the extension but didn't hold out much hope of getting one past eleven o'clock.

It came to the morning of the day when we were due to go to the magistrates, for the licence extension and I got a call from Roy's wife saying that he was ill. No one else who was in a position to act on behalf of the club was available to attend the hearing, so here I was, a few months after being convicted of drink driving, returning to the same court to ask for an extension to the club's alcohol licence. Roy's wife reassured me that it was very simple and they'd quickly say yes or no.

I trundled off to the court feeling reasonably relaxed and sat at the back waiting for the magistrates to appear.

'Will the court all rise.'

The rear door behind the bench opened and three magistrates appeared. I felt the colour leaving my cheeks as they took their seats. It was the same three who had heard my drink-driving case just a few weeks previous. I slumped down in my chair, trying to be as inconspicuous as possible and waited as the clerk of the court read out the applications for extended licenses.

'A twenty-first birthday party at The Red Lion on 20 November. Extension until midnight has been applied for.'

'Unnecessary, I feel', said the main man on the bench. His cohorts either side nodded in agreement.

'No.'

'A wedding at the White House Restaurant requires an extension until 1 a.m.'

The three on the bench huddled together in brief discussion.

'No.'

This continued along the same vein with every application. I realised that mine would undoubtedly end up on the same refused pile.

'Camberley Town Football Club have requested an extension of one hour for a pre-marital stag party. Their normal license only extends to 8 p.m. so this would mean an extension until 9 p.m.'

The main man on the bench looked up from his notes and said, 'Is there a representative for Camberley Town Football Club here?'

With heavy heart I stood up. The magistrate glanced down the courtroom at me, then did a double take. I just stood there, waiting for the refusal, but it didn't come.

'And your name and position within Camberley Town Football Club?'

'My name is Mr Wakeman and I'm the chairman.'

'May I ask who the extension is for?'

'It's for me, your honour.'

His eyebrows lifted.

'Could you please explain to me why do you need any extra

time for the consumption of alcohol above the normal granted licencing hours, Mr Wakeman?'

I explained politely that I had a lot of people travelling from various parts of the country and some wouldn't be arriving until mid-evening and some would in fact not even arrive until after the bar had shut.

The magistrate then addressed the court sergeant in attendance and asked him what sort of disciplinary record football club currently had.

'Since Mr Wakeman took over as chairman of the club we have certainly noticed a decline in juvenile crime. The club tries to attract as many youngsters down to the club as possible and that certainly has helped us considerably. Also, the club has had no instances of having been visited by police for any drinking offences either, your honour.'

The magistrate turned first one way and then the other to confer with his fellow court officials. Eventually he turned to face the front again and addressed me directly.

'Do you think an hour will be enough?'

'Pardon?'

'I said, do you think an hour will be sufficient for you to entertain your friends? If some of your guests aren't arriving until 10 p.m., they won't get a celebratory drink at all.'

He had one last conflab with his fellow magistrates, turned to me and said, 'Extension granted until 2 a.m.'

I was dumbstruck.

As was everybody else in the courtroom.

I walked over to the desk to collect my certificate and stood there waiting, the sergeant leaned across and said, 'Rest assured, Rick, we will be coming down on the night at exactly 2 a.m. and will stay as long as necessary.'

'Okay, fair enough – I presume this is to make sure it finishes?'

'Oh no, it's to make sure it carries on!'

CAVING IN AND TEE-ING OFF

By 1985 my drinking days were over and everybody said to me, 'What you need to do is find a hobby to occupy your leisure time and keep your mind occupied.' For some unknown reason, someone suggested DIY and for some other unknown reason I thought I'd give it another go. I say 'another' go because it has to be said that my one previous effort up until this point had not exactly been an unqualified success.

It was 1972 and we had moved into a beautiful detached house in Gerrards Cross. It had a very nice kitchen that adjoined the breakfast room. All the rage back then were can openers that attached to the wall and so I bought one. They are very simple to fix to the wall and I felt perfectly able to accomplish this simple feat myself, so I searched for my tool kit.

After about half an hour of thorough looking, I remembered that I didn't actually have a tool kit and so walked into town to the ironmonger's to rectify the situation.

I returned by taxi as the collection of spanners, hammers, wrenches, screws, nuts, bolts, tape measures, saws, spirit levels and screwdrivers, along with a very large tool box, were too much for one person to carry.

I put on the new overalls that I had also purchased, as I felt that if I looked the part then that would undoubtedly help the job go smoothly.

There was a small back piece of the wall can opener that needed to be screwed to the wall. It required four screws. I marked the places where the four screws would need to be screwed in and tried to screw them in directly. They wouldn't penetrate the plaster.

I took one of the small hammers out of the tool box and a large six-inch nail and proceeded to use said implements to make a small hole in preparation for the screw.

Unfortunately it made a large hole.

Undaunted I moved on to the second screw and again finding it impossible to screw it directly into the wall (I had never heard of Rawl plugs), used a slightly smaller nail in order to create the necessary starting hole. All this succeeded in doing was to remove a rather large piece of plaster.

I'm not one to give up and so looked for another area of wall close to the now destroyed area of wall, and tried again. By early evening I admitted failure and phoned a builder who came round the following morning.

He told me that with the damage I'd done there were two options. Either plaster the wall and redecorate or have a serving hatch. He recommended the serving hatch, as already there was daylight showing between the breakfast room and the kitchen.

Total cost if I recall was around £300, and this was 1972!

Actually the total cost was £301.50. (The extra £1.50 was for a hand-held can opener).

I tried a few other odd jobs but the problem was that my DIY was abysmal, shockingly bad. This wasn't because I didn't try, it was simply because I was just crap. I didn't have the right type of logical mind for it, I don't think. Let me give you some more examples.

When we moved into our new house in Norfolk in 2005, the

previous owner had stripped the place: they'd taken everything – he'd basically just left us some light bulbs and that was it. This was fair enough though because in the contract sale it stated very clearly that all the fixtures and fittings, carpets and curtains etc were not with the sale – however, it always comes as a bit of a shock to walk into a complete shell of a house when you move in.

In the kitchen, there were gaps all over the place where appliances had been, so I looked at this and thought this was my chance to get started on the DIY. In fact, this was DIY for beginners.

Quite simply, all I had to do was measure the gaps and then purchase appliances that would fit accordingly. No need for a hammer, or a drill or even a screwdriver.

I got my tape measure out and painstakingly measured every gap from every conceivable angle, then measured them all again and then once more for luck. Then I drove off into town to the electrical retailers and bought all sorts – a washing machine, a dishwasher, fridge, a freezer, all the stuff a kitchen could possibly need.

I had double- and triple-checked every measurement so it was easy to choose which appliances would fit. My fiancée, Rachel, was totally unaware of my previous DIY exploits and was very impressed at my efficiency. I beamed with pride. I'm sure the man in the shop was impressed too as I confidently referred to my notebook and then measured every appliance in sight with my tape measure, making notes along the way.

About a week later all the white goods arrived and the delivery guys began fitting them. They said they'd start off with the fridge. Five minutes later they came into the lounge and said, 'Mr Wakeman, the fridge doesn't fit the gap.'

'It must do – I measured that gap five times . . .'

I went into the kitchen and there was the fridge, clearly too tall for the gap. It didn't fit. What I'd done was measure to the top of the worktop rather than the underside, so that was mistake number one. And, of course, that applied to all the other machines as well. The delivery man said, 'Well, you could move the worktop up a couple of inches to fit the fridge in . . .'

'What a good idea . . .'

'But then your microwave won't fit on its shelf. Not that this will make any difference, because it doesn't really fit on there at present anyway.'

Great.

Suddenly, having bought four 'Easy to Fit' appliances, I was now in the middle of a major kitchen refit. Then I had a brainwave.

'Hang on – is the fridge on wheels?'

'Yes.'

'I'll get my sledgehammer. Give me two minutes.'

So off came the wheels (and a fair bit of white plastic with them) and the brand-new fridge was rammed into this gap with much huffing and puffing. We were now stuck with this fridge for ever: it was never going to come out.

Which was unfortunate, because I then realised that I'd put the fridge right next to the gap where the cooker was supposed to go. As a result, we now have the world's most inefficient fridge and our shopping bills are sky-high because the food's always going off really quickly. Plus we are the proud owners of an oven that takes eighteen hours to cook a roast because the right-hand side is stone cold as it's next to the freezer.

'At least we have the microwave, eh?' said a hopeful Rachel.

Well, not really. Since I'm six foot three, I hadn't considered that Rachel – who is only five foot two – wouldn't be able to reach up to the new higher shelf. She could just about reach when I got the stepladder out of the shed. (We actually don't use the microwave any more. Never liked them anyway.)

At least we had no such problems forcing the dishwasher in. According to my measurements, there was a beautiful one-inch gap all the way around, perfect.

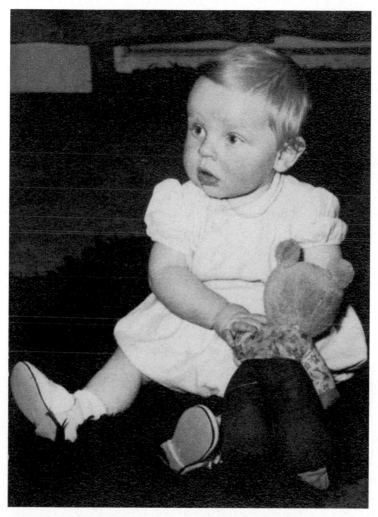

I wish I knew where my teddy ended up!

Me and my good friend Robin Gibb who took over the presidency of the Heritage Foundation after my term in office.

This was when I did the televised celebrity golf in Northern France. From left to right there Tony Jacklin (well a bit of his back and head anyway), one of the caddies, Bill Cotton Junio Kevin Keegan, another caddy, Ronan Rafferty, Sam Torrance, me and the cameraman who two holes later, I hit on the head with my tee shot and watched being taken off to hospital

From left to right: me, Ian Freeman, Robin Gibb and his wife Dwina at the
unveiling of the plaque for Alan 'Fluff' Freeman.

I love this photo of me as a toddler
as that is the nickname Rachel calls me –
and she's the only one allowed to!

Yes, I was fit once. This was taken at the registration for an Isle of Man fun run
more than twenty years ago! From left to right Jemma, Ben, Oscar and me.

Wendy Richard, June Brown and me.

Me in Cuba
with the statue of
John Lennon.

Taken at the opening of the Roy Castle Lung Cancer Institute in Liverpool. From left to right: Jean Boht, Sylvia Ingham, Ken Dodd, Fiona Castle, Stella Vaughan, Janet Brown, Frankie Vaughan, Cliff Richard, me, Robert Powell.

Me and Norman Wisdom having a cream bun fight! As this photograph shows …
Norman won!

Adam, Bonnie Tyler and me.

Except when they slid it in, there were at least five inches on either side. Minimum.

Almost enough room to put a microwave in.

I had also ordered a large television which I reckoned (I had measured very carefully) would fit perfectly in a gap between two shelves in the lounge.

It didn't.

A carpenter was called to realign the shelves and a plasterer to re-plaster the area ruined by realigning the shelves and then a painter to paint the entire room because we couldn't match the original colour.

The washing machine wouldn't fit in the utility room at all and now sticks out so the door won't shut. The cooker ran on Calor gas and leaked gas for the whole of its life up until a new kitchen was fitted, and guess what? I wasn't allowed to go anywhere near the new kitchen from day one when it was measured until the day it was completed!

I should have known DIY was not a good idea. There were plenty more precedents for my failure. In the 1980s we had moved into a beautiful old Victorian house in Camberley and although the kitchen was fine (by this I mean all the appliances fitted as they'd come with the house), there was a shortage of shelf space and so I decided to erect some shelves.

There were two wall cabinets with quite a substantial space between them. A totally wasted space, I felt, not least because the area in-between would be ideal to put two shelves. I jumped in the car and shot off to the local B&Q and bought various lengths of plastic coated wood.

I measured the distances carefully and cut two lengths of shelving. After discovering I'd cut them too small, (obviously a faulty tape measure), I had a few more attempts. Then I went back to B&Q to get some more lengths of plastic coated wood shelving.

Eventually I finished putting the shelves up and if I say so myself, they looked pretty damn good. I placed cooking oils on the shelves along with a few other jars of stuff and thought I'd celebrate by cooking myself a bacon sandwich.

I put the bacon under the grill and went into the lounge to watch some television whilst the bacon was cooking. I didn't watch very much because my enjoyment of *The World of Sport* was shattered by the explosion.

Nobody had told me that if you erect shelving above a cooker and said cooker has a high level grill, that the rising heat produced is quite substantial. Add this to the fact that plastic melts at high temperatures and I had built a recipe for disaster. The heat from the grill had bowed the shelves which eventually came away from their mountings and crashed onto the red hot grill, pouring cooking oil everywhere, which dutifully exploded.

Full credit to the Fire Brigade who were on the scene within minutes. They read me the riot act for what I'd done. Quite rightly too. My sarnies were ruined. I'd overcooked the bacon.

Never daunted by the odd little setback, a few weeks later I decided to attempt that most sacred of DIY challenges: *building a barbecue*. I found an old buried water tank made of steel and thought how clever I was to recycle this and make a stylish hand-built barbecue. I put aside the whole of Saturday to complete the task and even got up excitedly at the crack of dawn to start.

It really was a brilliant piece of design. I turned the tank upside down and pushed it into the ground. I found some metal mesh and fixed that to the top to make a grill. Then I went to B&Q, bought some bricks and ready-made plaster, went home and started laying bricks around four sides of the up-turned water tank. It was going along a treat. Getting carried away, once the bricks were laid, I slapped on some Artex and made some very hypnotic swirling patterns all over the outside. It looked *amazing*.

Even the kids were impressed. It looked the dog's dangly bits, it really did.

I finished by mid-afternoon, which was perfect timing because then I had the chance to go down to the supermarket and get some charcoal and then bags full of sausages, burgers, chicken wings – the works. I must have bought enough food for a hundred and fifty people, I was so keen to try this creation out. I slapped the meat on the mesh and lit the charcoal.

There were two things I learnt that day which were really interesting.

First of all, I hadn't realised that there's one type of Artex plaster for interior use and a *different* type for exterior use. There's also the heatproof type as opposed to the non-heatproof. I'd bought non-heatproof interior-use Artex. I sat there with my kids and friends and watched as the Artex started cracking all over the barbecue, just like in a *Tom & Jerry* cartoon when Tom gets smacked over the head with a mallet.

The second interesting fact I learnt is just exactly how incredibly hot a metal tank can get on its way to exploding. I suspect the actual temperature that had built up inside the sealed, airtight metal tank over the thirty minutes since I'd lit the stupidly large amount of charcoal was easily in excess of a thousand degrees. The first worrying sign was when we all heard a strange bubbling sound echoing around inside the tank. Then a weird rumbling began. The hot air was rapidly rising in temperature inside the tank and had nowhere to escape.

I got the kids back in the house just in time.

It really was the most phenomenal explosion.

Apparently, they found chicken wings as far as half a mile from our garden and the left-hand panel of the barbecue itself landed eight gardens away.

Learn one thing from my experiences: if you give up drinking, *DIY is not the answer.*

* * *

I do enjoy my sports. Just before I tell you about my love of golf, let me take a quick diversion into the equally civilised world of tennis. Well, it was civilised until I got there. One day the phone rang. It was the boss of Olympus cameras who I still did corporate work with.

'Rick, do you want to go to Wimbledon? We've got a hospitality tent and it's great fun – why don't you come along? I'm going to pick up Alan Ball first in a limo then we'll come round to yours and head off to south-west London to meet up with James Hunt the Formula One racing driver at his house in Wimbledon for Pimms on the lawn and then toddle off over to our hospitality marquee at Wimbledon Tennis Club. There'll be loads of champagne from the minute you step into the limo. Once we get there you can go in the hospitality tent, if you want to watch a bit of tennis you can, whatever, and then we'll come home stopping at a few watering holes on the way – we'll probably get back around midnight. We'll be with you about nine in the morning. Is that appealing?'

How could I say no?

God knows what time the Olympus chairman must have left to pick up Bally: by the time they got to my house they were both already rat-arsed. We drove about two miles before we stopped at a pub that was serving breakfast, then piled back in the limo and drank some more champagne before going over to James Hunt's house with at least six further stops at watering holes along the way. He'd set a table with Pimms and champagne (I think there were two sandwiches) so we got stuck in to the booze and left the food then all jumped back in the limo to finally head down to the tennis.

It was after one o'clock in the afternoon when we finally staggered into the Lawn Tennis Club. We must have *stunk* of booze. Lunch was being served for various high-powered Olympus associates all there in their finery, so it soon became apparent that we were the token celebrities for the day, beautifully holding up our side of the bargain by making a complete spectacle of ourselves.

After a lengthy liquid lunch, James left to go home at about 4 p.m. I don't think he'd seen a single tennis ball being hit – he'd brought Oscar, his German Shepherd dog along for the day and it wasn't allowed in the actual club, whereas it was allowed in by the hospitality tents so that was where he stayed.

Now, I love my tennis (I actually won several tournaments as a schoolboy), but if the truth be known, I was just too pissed to see anything. Even if I could have found my way to a seat, I wouldn't have been able to follow a single shot. After another hour of drinking, I turned to Bally and said, 'I think I need to have a sleep, Alan. I'm off to find somewhere to have a nap.'

Bally said he'd come with me so we staggered off in search of a corner to fall into. We were both weaving along by the back of some rather large vans when this man suddenly appeared in front of us and spoke.

'Well, it's a beautiful day here in SW19 and I've just bumped into the England football legend Alan Ball. And he's enjoying the tennis and sunshine with the rock musician Rick Wakeman.'

We had absolutely no idea who he was or what he was talking about. Or why he was talking in such a strange manner to us.

'Hello, Rick . . .' he said.

I belched.

He looked a little startled but carried on undeterred with his rather forced conversation.

'So, Rick, how are you enjoying Wimbledon today?'

I belched again.

'Alan,' he said, turning to my equally drunken friend, 'which one of the many super matches have you seen today?'

'None of them.'

'Ah, have you only just got here then?'

'No, we've been here since lunchtime,' I interrupted.

'I started out at eight,' offered Bally.

'Oh, really? So why haven't you seen any matches yet, gentlemen?'

'Er, that's because . . .' I suggested, '. . . we are completely pissed.'

This guy looked like he'd seen a ghost and quickly said, 'Er, that was our live afternoon report from Wimbledon for the BBC. Now back to you in the studio . . .'

After more drinks and a couple of naps, I stumbled home at well after midnight to find my answerphone going ballistic with messages. There were calls from the BBC asking me to report in the next morning to explain my behaviour, messages from friends and family saying they'd heard it all and quite a few giggling congratulations from my rather more rock 'n' roll acquaintances.

It was the early 1980s and swearing of any kind on the radio was a grievous sin. But to be fair no one got sacked, no one got suspended even, and it was all fairly harmless stuff. In my defence, a few friends said that from the first second of the unscheduled interview it was obvious that we were both absolutely pissed as farts.

I never did get to see any tennis.

I took up golf quite by accident in 1984. I'd actually gone to buy a car but instead of coming home with a Bentley T-Type I somehow managed to come home with a set of Mizuno Silver Cup golf clubs instead.

A mate of mine called Peter Vernon-Kell had a car company near Esher and I'd arranged to look at this particular car. However, there was a crash on the M3 and I was late getting to Peter's. He'd had enough of waiting and as I parked I saw that he was loading his set of golf clubs into the boot of his car.

'What about the car?' I asked him.

'Bugger the car for now,' said Peter. 'I'm going to play golf first, otherwise I'll miss my tee-off time – you can jump in and we'll talk about the car later.'

When we got there we went into the clubhouse where Peter went to register only to be told that his playing partner had called in to say he would be late and so the tee time had been moved forward one hour.

'Great,' I said. 'We can drive back and look at the car.'

'I'm not driving back, I'm going to the driving range. Come along.' Peter grabbed a bucket of balls and headed for the driving range. 'So tell me about the car, then . . .' I said as I hurried after him.

'Bugger the car, let me hit some balls first,' said Peter, clearly fed up.

As he started hitting the balls, I couldn't have cared less about his efforts – I had no interest in golf whatsoever, really. I kept asking him about the car that he was going to show me until eventually he said, 'Listen! No, I'm here to play golf. Here's a club – grab some balls and have a few shots will you?'

Peter showed me how to hold the seven-iron with the basic grip and I took a few wild swings at the ball, missing it completely the first couple of times. Then I started to hit it all over the place – slices, hooks, scooping it up in the air, everywhere except where it was supposed to go.

Then it happened.

By the law of averages it had to happen, I suppose. I hit a beauty and the ball sailed away straight as an arrow. It was like the heavens opening, angels peering down through the gap in the white fluffy clouds, I'm sure I could hear choirs singing and trumpet fanfares . . .

'Come on, then, Rick, let's go and talk about that car . . .' said Peter.

'Bugger the car. Why can't I hit the ball again like I did a couple of minutes ago'?

'Because you need lessons. Go and see the pro. He may even be able to fit you in now You can have a lesson whilst I'm out playing.'

I went to see the pro and he booked me in later that afternoon. He also sold me a second-hand set of Mizuno Silver Cup golf clubs, a second-hand trolley with odd wheels and a really naff bag that was falling apart, but the whole lot only cost a hundred quid. After a few months of literally playing every daylight hour, rain or shine, snow or sleet, hail or heatwave, I'd presented three qualifying cards and therefore earned my first handicap, a meagre twenty-seven but a start nonetheless.

But prior to getting my handicap, out of the blue, I got a call from the Comedians' Golfing Society. I obviously hadn't played in any tournaments or against lower-handicapped players yet: I was just finding my feet. Literally – as I was about to find out.

I thought this would be a good laugh, playing a round with a bunch of comedians; they'd be laughing and joking all day long. How wrong could I have been? Comedians take their golf *very* seriously. I went along to the Foxhills golf course, a very salubrious club in the heart of the Surrey countryside. Foxhills (where I later became a member) was also in a totally different league to where I had been playing my golf up to now. The club professional was Bernard Hunt, the wonderful ex-Ryder Cup player.

I walked up to the clubhouse and met a few of the other players. The first thing I noticed was the quality of their gear. There were golf bags that looked like thousands of pounds' worth of hand-made leather craftsmanship; clubs that were technological marvels; and clothing that was clearly just the *right* style, colours and logo.

Meanwhile, I was standing there in a pair of normal shoes with a very scruffy bag, a second-hand set of clubs and a wobbly, odd-coloured trolley that altogether probably cost less than one of their shiny professional five-irons. I was introduced to my fellow players and we walked off to the first tee, which was at the top of a hill. It had been raining so we all had umbrellas too (Correction: *they* all had umbrellas). I was first off so I put my ball on the tee, settled myself into my best stance and took a swing.

The ball went ten yards and came to a rest.

However, with my normal shoes on and the tee being soaking wet, I went much further. At first it was hard to balance but as I slid faster and faster down the hill I got the hang of it and ended up zooming about eighty yards like some maniacal skate-boarder on grass. When they'd hauled me back to the tee, I went and bought some golf shoes – although I still came last.

After a few months, November 1984 to be exact, I was grad-ually getting a little better (I no longer fell over on the back swing), but my handicap had not come down at all. I was slowly mastering the irons although had yet to hit any of the low irons. A five-iron was the lowest numbered iron I could hit. I had three very shiny woods that looked like they'd never been used, which in fact they hadn't. They were there for show. I hadn't yet plucked up enough courage to hit a driver or three-wood yet.

Then I got a call from a great friend of mine called Miles Dawson, who was the managing director of Panasonic. Back in the 1980s Panasonic used to sponsor the European Open which was always held at Sunningdale and Walton Heath. I used to do some corporate work for Panasonic so I knew Miles and his team well. As I mentioned, it was November, and I'd been 'playing' for only a few months.

'Rick, I've got your Christmas present sorted!'

'Great! What is it, Miles? Another telly?'

'No, Rick, much better than that. It's a round of golf at Wentworth with Nick Faldo.' And with that he put the phone down.

When I eventually got hold of Miles later that day he explained that Nick had been away from the game for some time perfecting a new swing. Since he was a music lover and because of Miles's backing of the European Open, Nick had agreed to play a four-ball with myself, Miles and another guy from Nick's management company. At Wentworth – one of the most difficult courses in the world. I would be up against a man who was arguably the greatest golfer on the planet at the time.

No pressure then.

The approach to Wentworth is beautiful and on the many occasions I've played it since I always marvel at the majestic clubhouse and greenery. At the time, however, I was too busy crapping myself. I'd forced my clubs into the front seat of my Porsche 911. As I began to play more and more golf, I came to realise that this was the most impractical car and so sold it and went back to Silver Shadows! As I walked to the clubhouse I think I must have seen about five famous golfers practising. And everyone had the most immaculate gear and the most tailored, pristine clothes.

I knew that my bag was on its last legs and a flap had actually opened up in the bottom. So I grabbed my trolley and pushed the decrepit old thing firmly in to make sure it didn't fall apart any more. To a rock 'n' roller like me, the one pink wheel and one black wheel almost looked alternative-cool. But not to anybody else.

Miles took me to the putting green to meet Nick Faldo. Nick's a really big man and on a golf course he naturally has a huge presence so everyone was watching him practise. He was lovely and his warm chat relaxed my nerves a lot. Then Miles said, 'I've got a surprise for you, Rick . . . some of the caddies have stayed over after the European Open and so as a special treat for us all, Nick has arranged some top caddies too. Nick's got his own, of course. I've got Jack Nicholson's caddy, Nick's partner's got Tom Watson's caddy and you've got Gary Player's caddy.'

Great.

Long ago I'd met Gary Player but didn't cover myself in glory. I just hoped his caddy didn't know the story. Let me rewind and take you back to Sun City some years earlier. I had been booked to play for a week at the Sun City Complex in South Africa. I was following Shirley Bassey, would you believe. Sun City is a very luxurious complex, which included a golf course designed by Gary Player. I was never really much of a gambler and I was years away from starting golf, so to be honest I just sat by the bar getting pissed and occasionally fell into the pool. We had five days off before our first performance and there wasn't really much to do, so I settled into this routine that seemed to work for me. Drank all day, fell in the pool, sobered up, drank a bit more, did the show, fell in the pool, drank a bit more and went to bed. That's what the band and crew did – there wasn't much else to see or do. Except they had an elephant there that used to play the slot machines.

Anyway, one day I was at the bar getting thoroughly rat-arsed and this guy came and sat next to me. 'I'd like to introduce myself. I'm Gary Player.' Now, golf is a life's passion for millions of people and it is also one of those games that if you don't like it and don't watch it on telly, its stars mean nothing to you. You can't avoid knowing some famous footballers, for example, even if you don't watch the game, but golfers weren't the same back then. So as I sat at the bar in Sun City, next to the living golf legend that was Gary Player, I'd never heard of him.

'Hello, Gary, my name's Rick Wakeman.' He seemed like a nice fella so we chatted and after a while, he said, 'I designed the golf course here, The Gary Player Country Club. It's only just finished. Rick, how'd you like to learn to play golf whilst you're here. I'll organise everything. By the time you leave here you'll have a handicap. The pro shop can kit you out with everything you'll need.'

'Oh, well that's really kind of you, Gary. Thanks for the offer, but it's not really my cup of tea,' I said, oblivious to the Golfer's Golden Ticket that I was just being offered. Gary nearly fell off his stool but, like I said, I was just not aware of who he was and I had no interest in learning to play golf and wasting valuable drinking time.

'Okay,' said Gary. 'Fair enough. I'm here if you change your mind.'

'I won't, but thanks ever so much.'

'So, Rick, what are you going to do to occupy yourself for the rest of the week?'

'Drink. Jump in the pool, drink some more, then play a show before drinking again.'

'Look, you come with me and by the time you head home. I promise that you'll have a handicap.'

'I've already got one of those, Gary: Not enough hours in the day to drink, party and make music.'

I never saw him again. And this must surely be one of the biggest errors I have ever made in my life, and so, on the off chance that Gary ever gets to read this, then I hope he will please accept the following personal note from my heart.

Dear Gary,

Your Highness, Your Lordship. How can I ever apologise for my appalling behaviour back in the early 1980s before I discovered the joys of golf. One lesson from you back then could have changed my life. One lesson from you now could change my swing, my hook and my abysmal putting. So, if you can find it in your heart to offer help to a much older and wiser rock 'n' roll fanatical golfer (handicap 13), then I will humbly fall at your feet in deepest gratitude, but I fully understand if you're too busy.

Yours, grovelling to the extreme,

Rick Wakeman

So fast-forward to my round of golf with Nick Faldo and I'm not in a hurry to meet Gary's caddy. As it turned out, he didn't seem to recognise me so I got away with it. Sort of. He came over and introduced himself and asked me where my clubs were. What followed next was just like a scene from *Only Fools and Horses*. John Sullivan couldn't have scripted it better.

I simply looked over by the putting practice area where a line of very expensive trolleys were parked. Mine rather stood out. It was like Del Boy's three-wheeled Reliant Regal parked amongst a fleet of Rolls-Royces and Porsches.

'It's the red, blue and green trolley with the black wheel on one side and the pink wire wheel on the other.'

All eyes around me seemed to be fixated on this multi-coloured golfing apparition.

'It's the one with the bag on it with the cover missing,' I added, in case he hadn't spotted it. To his credit he said nothing but simply walked up to the trolley and pointed at it.

'That's the one,' I said, smiling sweetly back at him.

'I'll carry if that's okay with you, Rick?' he said and before I could warn him he had lifted the bag off of the trolley.

Now golf courses are very sedate and quiet places and the only sounds that could be heard up until that moment were that of putters gently hitting balls on the practice putting green. Unfortunately, when describing my equipment to my caddy I had neglected to tell him that there was indeed no bottom to my bag as it had ripped and was now acting as a flap.

All fourteen clubs fell out of the bottom onto the concrete path and about fifty battered golf balls bounced down the hill. My caddy was left holding a very dilapidated bag with the bottom flapping away like a giant puppet's mouth from some kids' TV programme.

Wentworth came to a standstill. People had come out of the clubhouse to see what on earth was going on for themselves.

To his credit yet again, my caddy simply bundled the clubs up in his arms and walked off to the caddy hut where a few minutes later he emerged with a proper bag over his shoulder with my clubs in them. We all then trooped off to the first tee.

I could see Nick was more than a little concerned but he was being ever so friendly. A crowd of about two hundred people had gathered at the first tee because the rumour that Nick was out on the course had spread and he hadn't been seen for a long time. I was looking at this first hole and couldn't believe how long it was. I could hardly see the flag. I'd never seen a course like it. Nick walked onto the tee, teed his ball up and hit it. I don't think I had ever seen a projectile go so far. It was like a bullet, perfectly straight, amazing. He hit it further than I went on holiday. I say hit it, murdered it would be more accurate. I stood watching with my mouth gaping wide open.

The crowd applauded.

By now I'm just shitting myself, thinking, *This is just awful. I shouldn't be here.*

'Miles, you still got that wicked hook?'

'Yes, thanks, Nick.'

'Well, I'll give you all a shot a hole then,' said Nick.

A shot a hole? You must be joking. Ten shots more like!

Now Miles was a very good friend and I would never wish him any ill, but I hoped deep down inside that he would hook his ball as that would surely take some of the pressure off me when it came to my turn. Sadly, Miles let me down. He probably hit the best shot of his golfing life.

'Well done,' said Nick.

The crowd applauded.

Then the chap from Nick's management office stepped onto the tee. I noticed he had some sort of limp and then I realised as he walked past me, that he actually had a false leg.

Thank God! A chance! Three cheers for false legs! All hail Bob Flett! Miles is lumbered with me and Nick has got golfing's Long John Silver.

Long John teed his ball up, took the club back slowly in a lovely movement (*Nice swing*, I'm thinking), and then with controlled, almost robotic precision, the ball flew off like a missile, dropping only about ten yards short of Faldo's.

The crowd applauded.

'Amazing,' I said as he walked past me to the side of the tee. I admit to being not a little bit miffed.

'Well, actually Rick, the false leg's rather helpful. It never moves and I've adapted my swing around it so it's like a perfect base from which to hit the ball.'

I'm really pleased for you . . . not.

So now it was my turn.

How I held the cheeks of my arse together is beyond me.

Looking back, I suppose I should just have hit my favourite five-iron gently down the centre of the fairway, taken it easy and got away safely. But the pressure was simply enormous and, with at least two of the shots having travelled to different counties, I looked across at my caddy.

'Driver please,' I said.

The caddy handed it to me. A fine specimen of a driver. Ten-degree loft and in pristine condition. This was simply because I'd never used it before. I'd never even held it before.

Miles said that what followed was one of the most unbelievable scenes he'd ever witnessed in his life. I teed the ball up and as I addressed it, I was physically shaking as though I was holding a pneumatic drill. Due to my extreme nerves, I don't remember much after that so Miles filled me in later. 'Everyone went very quiet and you actually swung the club vertically over your head like you were holding a pickaxe. Then you came down with a slicing motion, like you were trying to decapitate someone. As it completed its downward trajectory, the bottom of the club hit the top of the ball. We measured the distance, Rick. It went four inches. Backwards.'

I do remember that part. And I also recall the next part when I kept the driver gripped in my hands and swung wildly again at the ball, only to see it roll eight yards down the main tee onto the fringe of the ladies' tee.

The crowd did not applaud.

In fact they simply stood in silence wondering what on earth was going on. Was Jeremy Beadle involved perhaps?

The battle between common sense and pride now took hold.

I was truthfully nearly in tears. I knew the sensible thing to do was to ask for my trusty five-iron and hit the ball down the fairway and take it from there. So I looked across at my caddy and said 'Five-wood please.' I realised my mistake immediately but it was too late. He handed me my five-wood. Another pristine club that had never been used or held.

I smashed the ball as hard as I could. It started off well enough but I'd obviously sliced it quite badly because it started heading right. Violently right and eventually the oncoming wind caught it and the ball started returning towards us, albeit twenty yards to our right. It hit a bank and flew onto the road where it bounced merrily away from the clubhouse until finally coming to rest in some bushes about a hundred yards from the first tee.

There was no applause.

Everyone else started walking up the first to follow Nick while I trudged backwards down the road to the bushes. Strangely, being alone with the caddy without all the people around had a comforting effect on me and I started to feel a whole lot better. We found my ball and I asked him what he thought was my best option from where I was. After all, that's what professional caddies do.

He looked at me, then the ball, and then down the fairway. Then he spoke.

'Okay, Rick, you are now a hundred and twenty yards further away from the hole than when you teed off. You've also played five shots if you include your penalty shot, so you're now playing six on a par four. Nick will undoubtedly birdie this hole. (That's down in three for you non-golfers.)

'And so your advice is?' I tried to sound as professional as I could.

'Pick up,' he said and walked off down the fairway to catch everybody else up.

I didn't get a lot better. I must have visited every bit of rough, every bunker, every out-of-bounds and every tree and bush on the course and a few others that weren't. At one point I'd taken about eight swings in the sand so I asked Nick, 'What do you recommend with regards to bunkers?'

'If you play golf like you do,' Nick said, 'don't go in them.'

Perhaps my most memorable round of golf – or rather, the most unforgettable – actually took place in Australia. A friend of mine called Peter Lister-Todd was the manager of the band Sky and occasionally they would take guest musicians out on the road with them when they were touring abroad. Rather nicely, they invited me to play seven shows Down Under with them. The money was rubbish but Peter sweetened the bad fee by saying he'd managed to get EMI in Australia to obtain entry to each of the seven prestigious Royal courses over there, normally reserved for professionals and elite club members only (I think the record label had shares or were involved financially in the courses in some way). 'If you think about it, Rick, it's a paid holiday – you play a bit of piano, then get to play golf on the seven Royal courses.' He knew he'd got me!

When we got to Sydney we headed for the course and the captain of the club, whom we were the guest of, handed me a huge sleeve of balls: there must have been thirty in there. I really couldn't see how I'd need that many, but he insisted. 'Trust me.'

On the first hole I hooked the ball left and my ball flew into some bushes. Thinking nothing of it, I was trotting off into the shrubbery to retrieve my ball when I heard a frantic shout. 'Rick! Get out of there quick!' The club captain literally pulled me out and said, 'Rick, there's brown snakes in there – very poisonous, mate.'

'How poisonous?'

'If one bites you and you don't have any antidote, you're dead in forty-five minutes.'

'And the nearest hospital with any antidote is . . .?'

'An hour away. Just drop a new ball down nearest the spot where your ball went into the rough with no penalty.'

I dropped so many balls – I was just terrified, looking for these brown bloody snakes. If my ball landed within twenty feet of a stick, I'd drop a ball. Some of these brown snakes were basking on the fairways and we were warned not to go anywhere near them. Advice we heeded!

We got to Canberra and EMI had arranged for me to play a round with the captain of the club there. Peter Lister-Todd couldn't make it as he had a business meeting so I was on my own. Normally that would've been quite an honour, but I'd heard that this particular tough old stick did not like Poms. The only thing he hated more than Poms was rock musicians. I began to realise exactly how much he didn't like Poms when the guy in the club-house who served me coffee beforehand said, 'You've got some balls, mate.'

I headed towards the first tee and this club captain was waiting for me, standing there looking pretty fierce. His opening gambit was, 'I don't particularly want to play with you, but it appears I have little choice so we're out in ten minutes. You a Pom?'

'Yes, and you must be Mr—'

'What do you do for EMI?'

'I'm a rock musician.'

'Right. Let's get this over with,' he said and marched off to the tee.

I hit a few decent shots and then hooked one into the bushes. 'I'm not going in there, I'm just going to drop—' I said.

'What are you talking about? Why?' the captain growled.

'Brown snakes!'

'Don't be stupid, we don't get brown snakes in Canberra. Bloody Poms. Go in there and hit your bloody ball. We're holding people up.'

A couple of holes later, I sent a ball crashing into a small cluster of trees and reassured that there were no brown snakes, I dived in to have a look. I quickly spotted the ball in-between two of the small trees and started walking towards it. It was then that I heard this kind of 'tut-tutting' noise.

Standing there, six inches from my ball, was a bloody great kangaroo.

I crapped myself, this thing was big. Gingerly, I held my hands up and walked backwards on to the fairway.

'I didn't see your ball come out,' said the captain.

'I haven't hit it yet,' I replied.

'Why not?' he stormed.

'There's a kangaroo in there . . .' I stuttered.

'Well, you're in Australia, what do you bloody expect, a four-eyed zebra with a dildo up its arse? It won't hurt you, just go back in there, push it out of the way and play your shot.'

When I went back in there, the kangaroo had moved and now his foot was actually on my ball. I was really frightened. The next thing I knew, this captain marched in, gave the kangaroo a little tap and this giant Skippy bounced away.

Things were not going well at all. We came to the ninth hole. To the side of the teeing area was the most beautiful blossom I'd ever seen on a tree. It really was spectacular, the colours were so vivid. As I stood there, the grumbly captain said, 'What are you looking at?'

'This tree, look at those flowers . . . just beautiful.'

The captain picked up a golf ball and threw it at the tree – at which point the 'blossom' revealed itself to be several thousand parakeets that flew away. The captain looked at me and said, 'Bloody Poms. That's the last bloody straw,' and as he stormed off the tee continued his rant. 'That just about does it for me! He thinks that parrots are flowers, he thinks we've got brown snakes in Canberra and he's only just discovered we have bloody kangaroos in Australia. I'm off.' With that, he stormed off towards the clubhouse.

When I eventually trudged my own way back to the clubhouse I went straight to the bar, in need of a very stiff drink, but couldn't have one because I'd stopped drinking three months previously so had to settle for coffee. The barman who'd previously served me coffee that morning poured me another one and said, 'What hole did you get to?'

'Finished the eighth and he buggered off on the ninth tee after a bit of a rant.'

'Really? You did very well – most Poms that play with him don't normally get past the third.'

'Really?'

'That's right. I thought you might have done better than most because the captain was in here a few minutes ago. Singing your praises he was, saying what a lovely fella you are.'

Don't you just love the Aussies!

BIRTHDAYS AND BIRTHS

I'm not a big fan of birthday parties. The reason I don't like birthdays is nothing to do with getting one year older, it's more the fact that I don't like there being one less birthday in your life. Plus, I've never really seen that many birthday parties go to plan. It's quite nice on tour because the crowd sometimes sing 'Happy Birthday' but otherwise, I'm not really a fan.

I only ever had one party when I was a kid and that was for my tenth birthday. To be honest, I think a lot of that was down to finance – in my younger days my parents had very little. However, when I was ten I was allowed eight friends over from school for a birthday party. We ate the usual jelly and sandwiches and cake but then it started to get a little bit out of hand. When my father arrived home from work, he reached the front gate at exactly the same time as Barry Sayers – with a dart stuck in the back of his head – was being led by two medics towards a waiting ambulance. I heard Mum in the kitchen in a terrible state, phoning Barry's mother and trying to explain why her little boy was having a dart pulled out of his head. I also remember her saying to my father, 'That's the last time Richard has a party here.'

And it was.

To be fair, there was great kudos waiting for me when I got to school the next day. 'Did you hear about Wakey's party? Barry Sayers got hit by a dart that went straight through his brain.'

Even for my twenty-first, I wasn't fussed, so I just went down to the Apollo pub in West Harrow and had a ploughman's and a pint with my good friend Dan Wooding.

However, there was one birthday celebration of mine that was extremely memorable, although I wasn't the central figure in what happened.

It was 1976 and I'd released a record called *No Earthly Connection*, which I then took out on the road. It was a stellar band, which included amongst others Tony Fernandez (The Greasy Wop) on drums, Roger Newell on bass, Martin Shields on trumpet and the great Ashley Holt on vocals. Amongst the remaining musicians was one particular gentleman whom I will give a pseudonym to for the purpose of relating the events of this particular evening and call him Roger Rivers.

Roger was somewhat older than the rest of the band and did his level best to keep us on the straight and narrow. We were all in our twenties but Roger was in his late thirties. He was a great musician and was known on tour as 'Dad' because he always used to say, 'Come on, come on, lads, early start in the morning. Off to bed.' We loved Roger to bits – he was a lovely man.

Roger had had quite a tough time. His first wife suffered from a very serious illness that sadly eventually took her life. We had an awful lot of admiration for Roger both as a person and as a musician and greatly admired how he'd kept going through what must have been terrible times.

In 1976 Roger was not in any relationship. We arrived in Hamburg as part of the German leg of the tour and it was my birthday. We were signed to Ariola Records over there, quite a big label. They wanted to take us out on the town and Hamburg is . . . well, let's just say Hamburg can be an interesting city to visit!

The record executives took us to one of the famous Hamburg clubs in the red-light district. Those of you who know about my visit to a red-light club in Holland (It's in *Grumpy Old Rock Star* – if your local store's sold out, maybe you could try Amazon) will also know these places tend to be very expensive if all you are actually after is a drink. There were women gyrating about the place and I seem to recall someone was doing something with a snake and a cucumber, but we were just after the booze. The English Rock Ensemble were notorious drinkers, as by now I'm sure you well know, and so when the Ariola bosses said the drinks were on them all night – we couldn't believe our luck.

'It's Rick's birthday! Champagne!'

As we were quaffing this bubbly, numerous voluptuous women were coming round offering various services but we were just interested in getting rat-arsed. That's what my band did. We never really had groupies as such, it was a drinking man's band. We were not pretty boys either so tended to attract the synthesiser brigade. No knickers thrown onto our stages, just synthesiser manuals! The type of music we played didn't really attract women either. Prog bands are notorious for 95 per cent male audiences and anyway we just wanted to get pissed. To be honest, if we were given the choice of either having some woman draping herself over us or playing darts with a pint, I think it would have been the latter every time. In fact I know it would, but maybe after the darts match was over . . .

While we were drinking this champagne chased down with extremely large Scotches there were a variety of acts on the small stage, all pretty soft titillation really. Then the record-company man pointed out that if you went into a cubicle to watch a sex show it was one price, but if you were willing to take part it was free. None of us were bothered and thought it was all an unwelcome distraction from bankrupting his record label with an appallingly expensive champagne bill. (I believe the final tally was over four thousand pounds – remember this was 1976.)

So we merrily carried on sinking bottle after bottle of bubbly when suddenly there was an announcement in German and then in English: 'Ladies and gentleman, we have a guest who wishes to perform for you with Marlene.'

This was just about enough for us to look up from our drinks in expectation of something memorable.

It was memorable all right, but not for the reasons we were thinking.

'Ladies and gentleman, all the way from England . . .' at which point 'God Save The Queen' came blaring through the sound system. All eyes were glued to the small stage as the curtains opened . . .

. . . And there was Roger, half-naked, with this busty Marlene sitting on top of him, gyrating and making erotic gestures. The stage set was decked out like a 1930's sitting room.

Roger could obviously see over the top of her gyrating body and at first looked stunned to see so many eyes staring at him! He looked across at all of us and these immortal words, that have since become legendary in the rock 'n' roll world, left his lips.

'Bloody hell, Marlene, what are all this people doing in my living room?'

We all stood up and cheered and the standing ovation lasted for a good five minutes.

It was priceless – we couldn't believe our eyes. Roger told us later that he'd gone into a cubicle by mistake thinking it was the loo and this woman had basically dragged him out and onto this settee behind a curtain. He thought, *Why not?* Then next thing he knew he was on a stage and we were all looking and howling over our drinks. Roger became a hero after that for quite some time. So that was one of my favourite birthday parties – good old Roger.

I have one last comment to make about birthdays. I made a decision some time ago when I was fifty-nine that when my sixtieth birthday arrived, I wouldn't be sixty, but start working backwards. In other words I would be fifty-eight again and the next year fifty-seven and so on.

I eventually reached this milestone and realised that if I went backwards I wouldn't get my heating allowance, free bus pass and free prescriptions, so I scrapped that idea.

I might not like birthdays, but I've experienced an unusually large number of incidents to do with births. For example, whenever I see an empty seat at a concert – which fortunately isn't very often – I think of Lancaster. There is a wonderful little theatre there called The Grand that is the third-oldest in the country, having first opened in 1782. The locals had raised all sorts of money to keep it open and had somehow managed to take over running it to keep it alive; however, they were always desperate for new funds and I'm always keen to support community theatre and have been a patron of several such places over the years. At the time, I only lived over the water on the Isle of Man so I happily agreed to play a charity show for them with my acoustic guitarist at the time, David Paton.

The stage was incredibly small, but the auditorium itself was a beautiful, ornate room. There was only enough room for two keyboards, David on a stool, and a very small PA but I didn't mind at all: I was eager to play the show and help out. So I was particularly pleased to find out before the show that they could have sold the theatre out ten times over due to demand.

However, when I walked on to the stage and started chatting with the crowd I noticed there was one empty seat. As I said, it was a very small auditorium so it stuck out like a sore thumb and I was obviously a little perplexed as they had a waiting list as long as your arm for any cancellations. So in the interval I asked the theatre manager about the empty seat.

'Ah, yes, well, all the seats were full, Rick, but just before the show started, we had a phone call saying that the wife of a gentleman in the audience had just gone into labour, that she'd been was rushed to hospital and he needed to go to her immediately.'

'Fair enough,' I replied, 'although it'd be really good if you could fill the seat for the second half – it just looks a bit odd.'

'Of course, Rick, we'll see what we can do.'

I trotted out for the second half and, sure enough, there was a man sitting in the previously empty seat. I did the show and afterwards there was a knock at my door from the theatre manager saying there was someone who wanted to meet me.

'It's the gentleman whose wife went into labour, Rick . . .'

'Oh, really? Has he just missed the end?'

'No, Rick, he was here for the whole of the second half.'

I thought, *Blimey, that's a bit quick*, so I invited him in. He was a very dour, very big Lancastrian. He shook my hand very firmly and said, 'Rick, pleasure to meet thee. I've always wanted to meet you and see you play live, especially in such an intimate theatre.'

'Well, that's really very kind of you, I'm really glad you enjoyed the second half. I hear your wife went into labour. Is everything okay?'

'Yes, fine. But I have to say she's a right inconsiderate cow.'

'Er, pardon?'

'Absolute total inconsiderate cow. She's not due for another two weeks and she knew how much I wanted to come to this concert. She can't stand you – she only likes something to dance to and I'm not a dancer and she said you've got to be epileptic to dance to Rick Wakeman's stuff. Plus she couldn't go anywhere because she's too fat, so I was coming here on my own, it was going to be a lovely night. I'm here one minute before you go on and the inconsiderate cow goes into labour. I cannot believe it. I'm convinced she's bloody done it deliberately.'

'So what happened?'

'I went along to the hospital and she was in labour and I said,

"Now look, you've got forty-five minutes to give birth. That gives me fifteen minutes to get back and see the second half."

'Impossible.'

'Not when you're in a hurry. She had a little girl.'

'Lovely.'

'Yeah, lovely. I'm proud of them both and love them both to bits. It's just her rotten timing, I suppose. Anyway, listen, Rick, what did I miss in the first half?'

I told him what I'd played and said that as I'd got more shows coming up quite locally, he should come along with his wife as my personal guest.

'That's really very kind of you, Rick,' he replied and off he went.

About two months later this couple came along to another show nearby. Afterwards I got to meet his wife and she was a lovely lady. He shook my hand really firmly again and said, 'Great show, Rick, really enjoyed it.'

'Thank you, really glad you came.' Then I turned to his wife and said, 'You didn't enjoy it, did you?'

'No, I didn't, no. I like something you can dance along to and your stuff, Rick, well, you'd need to be—'

'I know, yes, epileptic . . .'

She nodded politely.

'Listen, I hope your little new arrival is doing really well and any time you want to see another show, you are most welcome, just let me know.'

'Well, I'm sure *he* will, Rick, but if you don't mind, I'd rather not.'

I've been involved in births on other occasions. After most shows, people will come up to you and invariably their daughter's boyfriend is in a band or they themselves are in a band. They give you a CD and ask you to have a listen but the problem is, if I did that I'd have no time in the day to do anything else! But you try to listen and be encouraging as best you can.

One evening after a show, I'd noticed this lady with a man trailing a couple of paces behind her, with two children about eight or nine years old alongside him. There's a certain type of *hovering* – I knew they were waiting for me. I looked over and smiled and they came across and said 'Hi'. She explained that she and her husband had met at one of my concerts many years ago.

'Oh, that's lovely, glad I could help,' I replied, genuinely pleased.

'You did more than that, Rick,' she continued. 'We actually got engaged at one of your concerts too.'

'Oh, that's splendid! Lovely to hear.'

'And when we got married, we actually walked down the aisle to your music.'

I'm thinking, *Crikey, I'm not sure I'm that good!*

'I'm very flattered, thank you. I feel very honoured.'

But there was more.

'When both Tommy and Louise were born, my husband videoed the entire births, everything, all whilst your music was playing.'

'What a lovely memory for you both,' I said, not entirely sure why she was telling me.

At this point the husband piped up for the first time, rather nervously.

'Although your music was playing during the births, other noises and screams obliterated quite a lot of the musical textures so I overdubbed your music again when editing. I hope you like the result.'

And with that, he gave me a VHS tape marked 'Tommy and Louise. The Births.'

'It's really very good quality. You can see the detail really very clearly.'

I didn't know what to say. What can you say to that?

Stumbling for words a little, I said, 'That's really very kind of you but I think this is probably something very special to you two.' *Phew, quick thinking, Wakey, well done.*

'Oh no, Rick, we feel like you are part of our family, you really must accept it with our thanks,' the woman said, undeterred.

Still stuttering somewhat I said, 'That's ever so kind, but I really do think this is something to treasure in the confines of your own family home. It's really very private.' I felt terrible because they looked ever so disappointed.

At that moment, Doom (remember Stuart Sawney? My keyboard tech) walked over.

'What's that, Rick?' he said, looking at the tape I was handing back.

'It's a videotape of their children being born, with my music in the background.'

'Really? What music have they chosen then? *Journey to the Placenta of the Earth?*'

They missed the joke completely and the woman said, 'No, it was mainly to pieces from *King Arthur.*'

I stifled a snigger, trying hard not to laugh and hurt their feelings, and after they'd gone said, 'Doom, that was a very special tape from their lives and I have explained how deeply flattered I am but that I couldn't possibly take a copy and invade their privacy by watching their children being born. You'd have done the same, Doom, surely?'

Doom paused, deep in thought. After a few moments he spoke. 'You're right Rick. I would have done the same, but I wouldn't have refused if they'd offered a video of the conception.'

NORMAN WISDOM

I say I don't like birthdays but to be fair, I did enjoy the party for my fortieth. It was on the Isle of Man and my dear friend Norman Wisdom brought the cake in, complete with his trademark trip followed by an acrobatic tumble while, of course, all the time managing to hold on to the cake.

Norman was a near neighbour on the Isle of Man so we became close mates – he is one of the loveliest men you could ever wish to meet. We actually got banned from going to pantomime at the Gaiety Theatre on the Isle of Man because we were too loud. Jeremy Beadle was starring in a fabulous production one Christmas and Norman and I went along to watch, but Norman decided it would be more fun to join in and at one point, Jeremy actually stopped the production and said, 'I can't believe what I am seeing here, but Norman Wisdom and Rick Wakeman are standing on their seats screaming at me!' It got wonderfully out of hand and we decided to go back again the following day, where we were very politely told it would be best if we went home!

There's a really interesting thing about Norman's comedy that most people don't realise: although everything he does looks very spontaneous and light-hearted, I can tell you from personal experience that *everything* is timed to perfection and rehearsed over and over again. How do I know this? Because on a couple of glorious occasions Norman asked me to be his stooge.

Both times Norman had a show coming up and I couldn't say yes fast enough when he asked me to help out. Being a big fan, I knew a lot of the material so I told him I'd be really easy to work with, 'Don't worry, Norman, I'll bluff my way through!'

'Oh, no, Rick, we can't have that,' said Norman. 'We'll have to rehearse: there's some really important timings that we need to get just so – it has to be immaculate.' Sure enough, when we did rehearse he'd say stuff like, 'Rick, walk over to the piano, count to six in your head then say your line.' I'd do as I was told but he'd say, 'Rick, you're counting too fast!' He was so particular.

What I loved more than seeing his show or even being his stooge, however, was seeing him use this amazing sense of timing in his everyday life. Over the years I was on the wrong end of a few of his pranks and gags, so you never quite knew if something he said in the morning was part of an elaborate plan to catch you out later that night; it was most unsettling in a brilliant way.

One day my phone rang at home. I answered and it was Norman, who was whispering. 'Rick, hello.'

'Hello, Norman—'

'Ssshhhh! Listen, Rick, I need a favour.'

'Anything, Norman, just name it.'

'I want you to shout out the word "Bollocks".'

'Pardon?'

'Just shout out the word "Bollocks", please, just do it for me and make it really angry.'

Nothing surprised me with Norman, so I pulled my mouth away from the phone and shouted, 'Bollocks!'

'Ah, thanks so much, Rick,' said Norman, and put the phone down. Just as I put my receiver down, the doorbell rang and I went to answer it. My mind moved on to other things and it was only about three hours later that I sat down with a cup of tea and recalled the phone call from Norman and wondered what on earth it was all about.

So I rang him at home.

'Norman, what was all that about?'

'Oh right. Well, the vicar popped round this morning to see me about opening the church fete or something, and I made him a cup of milky coffee in one of my really nice bits of Royal Doulton. Anyway, I bloody well dropped it, didn't I? On the stone tiles in the kitchen floor! Smashed it to pieces. Now, I could hardly swear in front of the vicar, so I thought I'll call up my mate Rick and he can do it for me. And you did. Thanks Rick.'

'That's bollocks, Norman,' I said trying hard not to laugh.

'I know,' he said, laughing down the phone. 'Thinking about it, I would have said "Shit!"'

Norman and I regularly used to go to a lovely old-fashioned café in Peel on the Isle of Man for a bit of lunch and a catch-up. Norman loved runny egg and chips, and the bread had to be cut into soldiers. We used to chat and laugh non-stop – I loved those lunches. Mind you, I don't think I ever saw Norman's wallet: he'd always pat himself down and say, 'Rick, I've brought the wrong jacket, my wallet's at home . . .' with a really cheeky grin on his face.

Now to say Norman is the most loved person on the Isle of Man would be to put it mildly. He is *adored* by the Manx people and quite rightly so. He's been over there for decades. He basically went over there to star in a pantomime and loved it so much that he built a house and stayed there. The people love him and he's been a great ambassador for the island – he supports everything. He opens fetes, garden parties, new buildings, you name it, Norman's probably opened it! In fact I have heard it said that the only thing he hasn't opened on the Isle of Man is his next-door neighbour's mail. There are bronze statues of him all over the island and so there should be: he's done a lot for a lot of people, not just on the Isle of Man but all over the world.

One result of his legendary status over there was that whenever he walked into a shop *everyone* would stop what they were doing. Now, Norman would talk to anyone but the Manx people were always good at keeping a respectful distance – they never invaded his privacy (or mine for that matter). But even though they might not intrude they would earwig, because Norman was always hot news. Norman being Norman, he sometimes used this for a little bit of cheekiness.

One particular afternoon, we were sitting in our favourite café with our egg and chips, soldiers and mugs of tea. The café was busy with quite a few elderly ladies chatting over their lunch, but we were being politely left alone as usual. At this time Norman and myself were both coincidentally looking for new secretaries, so that became the main topic of conversation.

A little louder than he needed to speak, Norman said, 'So, Rick, how are you getting on with your search for a new secretary?'

More than a few pairs of ears pricked up in the café but it was barely noticeable. I explained to Norman that it was more of a PA/secretary that I was after and most probably the ideal candidate was someone who had some experience of the entertainment industry.

By now the entire café had stopped their own conversations and were all listening to ours.

'Because the thing is, Norman, I work weird hours: sometimes I'm abroad and might need the office to be open while I'm in Japan and it's the middle of the night in the UK. So it's tough, Norm, because I need somebody who is happy to work incredibly flexible hours. I need a lady with a very understanding husband who can recognise this is not a nine-to-five job. How about you, Norman, how are you getting on?'

You could almost taste the anticipation as Norman began to speak about his search for the perfect middle-aged, doting, helpful secretary.

Forks in elderly female hands were held in seemingly suspended animation as they concentrated on hearing Norman's answer.

'It's a nightmare for me too, Rick . . .

'She's got to be really multi-purpose because, as you know, I live on my own in that big house so I need someone who can look after the office, be in touch with London and organise my trips backwards and forwards, but also look after me and my house.'

There were understanding nods at the other tables. Everybody knew Norman's house and everybody knew how much he crammed into his days.

Norman continued in a similar vein saying how demanding the job looking after him was and the knowing glances and nods from all the elderly ladies at the other tables told us that they were both fully sympathetic for Norman's plight, but more importantly, were listening to every word that Norman spoke. As Norman continued speaking, we got up from the table and walked up to the till.

'I'm nearly eighty now, Rick, it's a very demanding job for someone . . . hang on, Rick . . .' He patted himself down. 'I seem to have brought the wrong jacket.'

'No problem, Norman,' I said. This was the usual situation at the counter after our lunches. 'I'll sort it.'

Norman continued talking whilst I asked for the bill and his uninvited audience were still hanging on to his every word.

'So you see, Rick, the woman I'm looking for really has to be an experienced all-rounder and be prepared to do most things and – he now paused for dramatic effect – 'I'd also like to think that the occasional shag wouldn't be out of the question,' and with that he walked out the door.

His timing was pure genius. I was still in the shop and looked round at these 'ladies who lunch' and the looks on their faces were amazing. Mouths gaping open, sharp intakes of breath – one lady even took a half-eaten sausage off of her fork just before it was about to enter her mouth.

They were also looking at me as if *I'd* said it, so I paid up and slouched out, shoulders hung low as they tutted at me. I got outside and there was Norman, waiting for me, laughing hysterically. I just shook my head, burst out laughing myself and said 'I think you might have one or two more applications this afternoon, Norman.'

It's widely known that Norman Wisdom is a national treasure in Albania. This is not an urban myth, I've seen it in action with my own eyes. The Grand Order of Water Rats, of which I am a very proud member, organised a ninetieth birthday party for Norman and basically the entire government of Albania came over to honour him. In Albania they have cinemas devoted to screening Norman Wisdom films all day, every day. It's all down to the fact that when Albania was very much a downtrodden, poverty-stricken Eastern European country, Norman's movies were the only Western films allowed under the rule of the dictator Enver Hoxha. His films portrayed the life of Mr Pitkin – the poor, downtrodden little worker. The entire nation took him in as their hero, a symbol of the underdog who could beat the system and the big nasty bosses of this world. Norman is greeted as a super-celebrity whenever he travels there; when the England football team travelled to play there in 2001, the Albanian government insisted that Norman went over with the squad.

When the plane carrying the England team landed in Albania, there were thousands and thousands of people at the airport. Our footballing heroes were suitable chuffed at such a turn out until it became clear that they were there to see Norman. The England football team were a total irrelevance!

At the training ground, while David Beckham and Co. were largely left to their own devices, Norman was mobbed. At the time, he was eighty-six.

Perhaps my favourite Norman Wisdom event happened during one of the many times we played golf. It was one of the most hilarious rounds ever. It was a four-ball with myself, Norman, Christopher Strauli who played Norman Binns in that fabulous sitcom *Only When I Laugh* and Garfield Morgan who played Hoskins in *The Sweeney*. Norman was well into his eighties by this point and when we arrived his then-PA was there, looking quite concerned.

'Norman is not to walk the course, gentlemen, he is not fit enough to walk round eighteen holes,' she said. That was fair enough so we went and hired him an electric buggy. Norman started to do his 'little boy lost' impersonation – 'I don't want to go in the buggy' – but the PA refused to leave unless he used it – 'on doctor's orders' apparently. He finally relented and she was really pleased. Norman watched her drive out of the car park and off into the distance, then jumped into the buggy and drove it straight into the first bunker he could find, got out and walked back to the tee and with a wicked naughty boy smile on his face said, 'I can't use it now,' he said, 'it's stuck.'

The rules of golf go out of the window when you play with Norman Wisdom. Your own game suffers too because you spend so much time laughing that it's impossible to concentrate. All the way along he was doing his famous trips and twists and tumbles, and we were all in stitches. On one hole he hit his ball into a bunker and I thought my sides were literally going to split: he was hacking away, missing the ball, grumbling in this comedy voice, tripping, falling over, sand was spraying out everywhere – it was one of the funniest things I've ever seen. He spent about fifteen minutes slicing away at the sand and taking God-knew how many shots. We were in fits.

Eventually he got fed up so he picked up the ball and threw it on to the green. Then he took three putts to hole out and said 'Four!'

'That's not a four, Norman!' I protested. 'You must have taken twenty shots in the bunker alone!'

'Ah, but they don't all count.'

'What?'

'Well, you've heard of a Mulligan, haven't you?'

'You mean if a player hits such a bad shot off the tee his playing partners can let him start again from scratch without penalty?' I offered.

'Exactly,' said Norman. 'Well, those shots are covered by what is known as the Montgomery.'

'A what?'

'The Montgomery. Remember the war and Rommel? Well, with a Montgomery I can have as many shots as I like and when I finally get it out that cancels out all the shots that went on in there. So if you work that out, plus the fact that I didn't mean to hit some of those putts, it's a four.'

We were too busy laughing to protest any further.

Norman wrote down a four.

Norman was rightly knighted in 2000, apparently largely because the Queen Mum was a huge fan: she loved him to bits. Now, when you go to the palace to get an honour you are instructed on the stringent decorum and etiquette that is required when you are in the presence of the Queen. Comedians are given particularly strict instructions so that they are not tempted to stray outside the 'done thing'. However, there are two comedians who despite all the warnings, managed to add a little extra to the service when in the presence of Her Majesty: Norman Wisdom was one of them. (Les Dawson was the other!)

Norman went up for his knighthood and had a nice little chat with the Queen, whom he'd met before and who was also a big fan. Then he turned very deliberately and carefully and began to walk away. However, he couldn't resist and as he took another step, he did his famous little trip, looked back at the Queen and saw that she was laughing. Only Norman Wisdom could get away with that. What a lovely man – as the Albanians would say, he's a national treasure.

TELLY ADDICT: PART II

Although I love doing TV shows my appearances have not always gone smoothly. There are many fine examples of this apart from the *Mastermind* debacle. The next one that springs to mind is a TV quiz programme called *That's My Dog*, an absolutely appalling show made in Plymouth at TSW back in the 1980s. It was only really shown in a couple of regions outside of Devon and Cornwall. Border and HTV were the other two, if I recall. I'm surprised it was ever shown anywhere at all, to be honest with you. Whoever thought the concept up and then somehow got it on air . . . well, it's beyond belief, really.

There were two teams for each show, plus a live studio audience. The presenter, Derek Hobson, would come on and stand in front of a giant kennel. Then out of this fake kennel would walk a canine handler and a dog on a lead. Then each team had to ask questions and try to deduce from the answers who the celebrity dog-owner was. It was like *Through The Keyhole* only nowhere near as good. Or as popular.

They would literally look at the dog and say, 'Is Lassie's owner in the music business?' and the crowd would clap or not, depending on the mystery celebrity. And so on. Eventually they'd hazard a guess and once they had got the answer right the celeb would reveal all by walking through the giant kennel themselves. The dog would invariably jump all over its owner who would be licked them to death, the crowd would applaud and that was that. Quite appalling.

There were two dogs and two celebrity owners per show. During the ad break between the two dogs appearing, they would invariably have to clean up the little (or large) gifts that the first dog had kindly deposited on the floor. It was generally considered best to be on first if possible as the smell didn't usually quite set in until the second half.

So one day 'my people' got a call from the *That's My Dog* 'people'. Then they phoned up my office on the Isle of Man and said they really wanted me to go on with my German Shepherd dog Chloe. ('Because we've never had a German Shepherd on before' – no mention of any interest in me.)

I spoke to them on the phone. 'Okay. Well, she's a very well behaved ex-police dog that didn't quite come up to the required standard during training as a puppy, so I bought her. She has quite a history,' I explained, and I could hear the TV researcher getting rather excited. 'Yes, as I said, she didn't quite make the grade for active police service so we took her home and she's a lovely family pet and wonderfully obedient and has the most beautiful nature.'

About two days before I was due to set off for Plymouth from the Isle of Man, a journey that would require a four-hour boat trip and then an eight-hour drive with stops, the same researcher rang me back and said, 'Rick, we've got a big problem. We have to work closely with the RSPCA and they say there's no way they can sanction a dog travelling by car from the Isle of Man to Plymouth.'

'But Chloe comes with me everywhere – she drives miles all the time. Plus I always stop off and give her a walk.'

'Sorry, Rick, they won't allow it. The problem is, the programme is ready to be made and we've put so much work into it that we still want you to come on.'

'Me too? So what are we going to do?'

'Well, do you know anyone who lives near Plymouth who owns a German Shepherd that they can lend you?'

'What?'

'We were thinking, if you get a replacement dog that lives closer to the studio it'll all be sorted.'

This was nuts but it seemed the only way forward. As it happened, I had a mate called Ray who lived in Camberley and who had a German Shepherd that was the security dog for his builder's yard. However, whereas Chloe was a real softie, Ray's dog was a beast, a vicious attacking machine trained to bite and never release. No one could get anywhere near it except for Ray himself.

'Well, I do know someone with a German Shepherd who lives in Surrey, but his dog eats people,' I warned. 'He'd have to bring him.'

'I'm sure it'll be okay, Rick. Let's go with that.'

On the day of the filming I arrived at the TV station to find Ray there with his dog.

'We've got a problem, Rick.'

'What's that, Ray?'

'Well, your dog's a bitch and my dog, err, isn't. Anyone watching this is going to notice that your lady dog's managed to grow a dick.'

'You can't see a dog's dick normally,' I countered. 'So it should be okay.'

'What about his balls then? Are you going to pass them off as earrings that have slipped off his head?'

He had a point but we were too far down the road to do anything about it.

'We haven't got any choice, Ray.'

When the show's dog handler came to take Ray's dog it nearly killed him. So after we'd dragged it off and calmed it down Ray agreed to take the animal on set himself. 'For God's sake, keep that monster away from Linda Lusardi's Yorkshire Terrier!' the researcher shouted as this vicious dog dragged Ray off towards the studio.

I can't actually remember this dog's name, so let's tell it like it is and christen it Killer. The producer came over, looking a bit annoyed, and said, 'It's not a very friendly dog, is it? Everyone is terrified.'

'Look, I did warn you and I've done what you asked. I can't do any more.'

They miked me up and took me backstage to stand inside this giant kennel ready for the show to start. This was the day I learnt to always switch off *and* take off your mike when a show is 'finished' . . .

But I'll come to that. Let's get back to Killer.

The theme tune was playing and Derek Hobson walked out and started his chat. 'Today we have a beautiful friendly German Shepherd whose mystery owner is waiting backstage. This very special dog has come a long, long way to be with us today, all the way from the Isle of Man, so that's your first clue. Please welcome Chloe.' And with that the giant kennel door opened and Killer came out with Ray, tugging at his thick rope lead, snarling, salivating and growling nastily at anything that moved. He just went into killing mode: there were teeth bared everywhere, Ray was being dragged along like a rag doll, people were absolutely terrified – it was total mayhem. Eventually Ray got Killer sort of under control and the dog sat down.

At which point the beast started to have an erection.

So this lovely cuddly *female* dog, who would be far happier killing someone than appearing on a third-rate quiz programme, is now having a giant erection.

I can't remember if the two teams guessed it was me or not because that became immaterial. I do remember hearing the presenter saying, 'And now we will reunite this loyal, loving dog with its celebrity owner!' I walked through the giant kennel door and immediately realised it had been a mistake to wear a big leather coat – Killer sensed a victim and just went for me. He broke free of Ray's grasp and launched himself all over me, teeth gnashing wildly as I tried to keep him at bay with my hands around his writhing neck. As I tried to avoid being eaten alive, I actually heard the presenter saying, 'Ah, look at those two, Chloe's so pleased to see her owner. Playful little thing, isn't she?'

The audience were dumbstruck as Killer was eventually pulled off me and finally brought under control. I stood up, my leather coat and trousers were ripped and there was the odd spot of blood on the side of my cheek.

'So let's say goodbye to Rick Wakeman and his loving German Shepherd, Chloe.'

As we walked off, one of the audience leant over and said 'How come your girl dog's got an erection?'

Without stopping I replied, 'It's not an erection, it's a large wart.'

I did a final wave to at the audience, which Killer took as a signal to attack and once again he had me on the floor as the kennel doors closed behind me.

Ray finally pulled Killer off and I left the studio with my mike still switched on.

Backstage I walked into the green room and there was the lovely Linda Lusardi. 'Blimey, Rick, what's happened to you?'

'Long story.'

'Your dog didn't look very pleased to see you. And it didn't look very much like a girl either.'

Blissfully unaware that my mike was still on, I took Linda to one side and explained the whole sorry saga. To my surprise, she listened to it all then said, 'Oh, you an' all, eh?!'

'What do you mean?'

'Rick, I haven't even got a dog. They wanted some glamour on the show so they've give me this bloody yappy Yorkshire Terrier – he's horrible.'

Unfortunately, some mischievous spark in the control room was listening in and heard everything. The next day I found myself along with Linda on the front of one of the tabloids with the headline: 'That's Not My Dog!'

The programme was never aired.

While I was still living on the Isle of Man I got a call from Kevin Woodford, the television celebrity chef who also lived on the island. He had a new show called *The Reluctant Chef* which took celebrities with no cooking skills whatsoever and taught them a few tricks. The problem was, I actually loved cooking.

'Forget about that, Rick – for the purposes of this show you don't know anything!' he said, chuckling. 'All the programmes are filmed except one – we've done romantic dinners, we've done Sunday roast, breakfasts, picnics, the only thing left is barbecues.'

As you now know, I had form with barbecues but I agreed to do the show undeterred.

'Do you have a barbecue, Rick?' he asked.

'What's the fee?' I countered.

'Three hundred and fifty pounds.'

'When do you want to start filming?'

'Two weeks' time.'

'Then I've got a barbecue.'

Immediately after I put the phone down, I called a local builder friend and organised for him to come round and build me a barbecue in the garden. Amazingly it just happened to cost £350 too!

On the first day of filming Kevin sat down with me and explained the order in which he wanted to do everything.

'Rick, the important thing about barbecues is marination. This takes time and preparation. Therefore, we've got to buy the meat first, so the opening bit of filming will be at the butcher's shop in Ballasala. I've spoken to Henry the butcher and he's waiting for us.'

So off we drove to this small village in the south of the Island where Henry had one of the best local butcher's shops.

They set the camera up in the shop and Kevin asked me to walk in from around the corner, so off I toddled and waited for the signal to start walking. We waited until there were no cars passing and the signal came for me to set off, which I did. All you could hear was the sound of my shoes on the pavement, the odd bird singing and two very tuneful farts between my third and fourth and ninth and tenth and steps respectively.

Later I found out that the cost of overdubbing street sounds to block out the sound of my prodigious farting cost them quite a bit of money.

Twenty-four hours later, with the meat and other food well and truly marinated, we were ready for the barbecue itself.

Kevin was talking to camera saying, 'We have top quality local produce, it's so important for a good barbecue. Don't fall into the trap of buying cheap cuts.' As he spoke, I glanced across at the table and there was my German Shepherd dog Chloe just polishing off the last mouthful of the Island's finest organic, hand-reared meat.

We were running out of time now so we drove like lunatics to the local cheapo supermarket and all they had left were some very dubious cuts of their 'basics' range. We had no choice but to buy them, and we even managed to soak them in 'marinade' for about three minutes and cooked it all up on this barbecue.

We were then filmed sampling these delicious wares. 'Oh, Rick, can you tell the marinade has been left overnight? You can really taste the meat's juices responding to the process, it's superb.'

'Yes, Kevin, I see what you mean, ummm, delicious.'

'Cut!'

'Rick, what did you really think of it?' asked Kevin.

'It tasted like shit,' I replied, spitting out the last few bits of this foul meal.

Chloe wouldn't eat it either.

Some time in the early 1990s, I got a call from *The Travel Show*. They were running a feature where each week a guest presenter was sent on a holiday and reported back. I liked watching the slot myself so when they asked me I was delighted. I knew it was a lottery where you went – it could be Paris, Barbados or Whitley Bay – it was a bit of a lottery. I was convinced I'd be sent to Skegness or somewhere like that. The money was peanuts but I didn't really care. It was something I really fancied doing, wherever they sent me – I will wade through boiling oil to do TV. I said I'd love to.

'Great. Well, you are going to India,' the researcher said.

'You are kidding! Brilliant! I expect you've heard I like curry?'

'You're going to Kerala, to follow the spice trail,' she said.

I couldn't believe my luck. A free trip to India, as much curry as I could eat (or so I thought) and a TV show to boot. Brilliant. The idea was also to film a few of the colourful religious festivals and sample some authentic local cuisine, plus visit a spiritual area and a school of young students who apparently had yet to actually see a white person in the flesh. It was over a week's stay. I was just ecstatic – it was a dream, really.

'The only reservation you might have, Rick, is the internal flight you'll need to get from Bombay. The only airline that takes you down to the festival in southern India isn't exactly British Airways. In fact, they are not even accredited with IATA or any recognised safety body. We don't even know if they have a track record of crashes or incidents because no one's got any paperwork on them. So we can't confirm the rumour that they've run out of planes because they've deposited them all over southern India.'

I actually didn't care, I was so excited about the trip that wild horses wouldn't have stopped me going. 'Don't worry about that!'

I said and agreed to the whole thing, including the internal flight on 'Plummet Air'. To be honest, the closest I'd ever got to India was actually on British breakfast TV. It was 6.30 a.m. one morning and I'd found myself sitting in the *Breakfast TV* studios next to an old woman and a six-foot parrot. I was coming on the show to promote my latest record – they usually ran a book or record feature with guest appearances. The green room at Lime Grove where *Breakfast TV* used to be filmed, was very small and when I walked in I was delighted to see Graham Chapman and Terry Jones from *Monty Python* dressed as an old lady and a parrot respectively. We chatted away happily for over an hour or so and were looking forward to our slots when suddenly all hell broke loose. Researchers were running around, presenters were scrabbling through reams of freshly printed news flashes – it was pure chaos.

We knew something serious had just taken place and so sat waiting for someone to fill us in.

Finally Frank Bough, who presented the programme, poked his head round the door, looked at me and said, 'Rick, we've got a big problem, Indira Gandhi has just been assassinated.' He continued, 'I think it's very unlikely that we'll get an opportunity to get you on the programme, Rick, as this morning is now going to be very serious indeed, no light-heartedness at all as you can imagine. I'm awfully sorry.'

'Fully understood,' I said in a sombre tone.

At which point the parrot and the old lady looked up and said, 'So what about us, Frank?'

I know it was a very serious moment in history, but it was bloody funny. Those guys were comic geniuses.

So I was hardly an expert on the Indian subcontinent. Therefore the chance to visit the country in person felt like a lottery win. I woke up on the morning of the departure and I was so looking forward to the trip that even the flight felt like an excursion. *Air*

India to Bombay! They are bound to serve curry on an Air India flight – yes! Sure enough, we took off and after a couple of hours they started to bring the food around. One of the options was curry. I selected the curry and, so it seemed, did most of the other passengers. I tucked in and it was beautiful. Like a high-quality restaurant curry rather than the usual plane fodder.

I polished everything off, had a drink and then settled back into my seat to watch the film and enjoy the rest of the long-haul flight. As I did so, I noticed a steady stream of people walking up and down the aisle. Then I started doing the maths.

Over three hundred passengers on board.

At least two hundred and fifty of them ate the curry.

Ten toilets.

Bombay is a bloody long way from London.

The sums were not stacking up well. Even with the air-conditioning on the plane there was a certain familiar smell that was starting to linger.

I tell you what: the pressure that built up inside that cabin at 35,000 feet was phenomenal. I still maintain to this day that if they'd run out of fuel they could have opened the back up and the plane would have flown the last thousand miles on its own accord. *Mental note: do not eat the curry on the flight home.* It stank in there although I have to be honest here and say I could probably have single-handedly fuelled the plane from a hundred miles out.

When I got to Bombay in the early hours of the morning I really didn't know what to expect. Well, the culture shock hit me before we'd even left the airport – the amount of people sleeping on the floor was incredible, it seemed like there were thousands, just a sea of people. By the time you'd recovered your suitcase you then had to pick your way through these prostrate bodies, all asleep, before you hit the outside and the instantly suffocating heat even in the early hours of the morning.

I had instructions to head to a nearby domestic airport to make my transfer for the internal flight. I followed my instructions but couldn't for the life of me see any taxi or shuttle bus. Worse still, some ancient wrinkly old guy had parked his dilapidated death trap of a van in the space reserved for the shuttle.

This old guy looked over my shoulder and when he saw my paperwork he said, 'Welcome to Bombay. I take you to the other airport.' I climbed into this battered old open-backed van and the driver took my case for me. *Very good, nice to know my stuff's being looked after.* Then he put my case on an ox-cart which immediately headed off in a totally different direction.

We drove off and I tell you, I've never seen roads like it. I say 'roads' – they were just massive open spaces of tarmac with enormous potholes everywhere. Even at four in the morning, there were cars everywhere – how nobody hit anyone else I'll never know. There seemed to be absolutely no legal requirement to drive on any particular side of the road, avoid crashing or hold any regard for other road users or indeed for human life generally. The only road users who seemed to go wherever they wanted were cattle and other wildlife.

Eventually I arrived at the domestic airport, which was really not more than a few tin shacks and a strip of uneven grass and dirt. Amazingly, my case was already there waiting for me. I checked in and was directed to a small room overlooking the 'runway'. I was really interested because they'd sat me down near the emergency training area, it seemed, as there was a seemingly derelict, very early-model Boeing 737 sitting close to the window I sat by with what appeared to be severe black burn marks down the side, which I presumed was the result of successive fire drills. The tyres also looked very bald to me. I'm sure there were scorch marks around the engines too, so this was obviously where they ran drills and safety exercises. Given the researcher's concern about the airline, I was immediately impressed.

The room was slowly beginning to fill up with passengers. And ducks. And chickens. And a small goat. I stuck out like a sore thumb with my blond hair and being so tall. It was all fascinating, though: I was in my element.

Then a group of about thirty people were ushered in, looking around nervously and obviously very anxious. Most of them were clearly quite frightened. Then an announcement was made, first in Indian and then in English, that the plane was ready for boarding and that we should make our way to the gate. Taking one last look at the derelict shell of a 737 that they used for emergency training, I asked a nearby flight attendant where my plane was.

'Why, it's that one, sir,' she said and pointed at the scorched wreck of a plane outside my window. I looked around and there were the captain and the crew boarding this total shambles of a flying horror tube.

Having reassured myself that it couldn't be as bad as it looked, I stood up to queue for boarding. When they opened the doors to the runway it was like the start of the bloody London Marathon. Men with legs missing, women, children, chickens, ducks, every type of creature known to man seemed to be racing across the tarmac to get to the plane.

It was quite a race and I was quite pleased with myself. I came second behind an elderly lady with one eye. I climbed the rickety staircase and grabbed a seat by the emergency window. *If this rust bucket goes down, at least you're in with a chance, Wakey.*

I don't normally mind flying, but I have to admit that by now I was more than a little worried and the curry from the Air India flight hadn't entirely left my body either.

I looked around this plane and I have to admit it was terrifying. It smelled – really smelled. There were seats missing – there were entire *rows* actually *missing*, luggage compartments were half-hanging off the ceiling, and there were even some loose cases lying on the floor where there should have been seats. I was in a row of two seats. There should have been three but the aisle seat was missing. There were however three of us in this row. Myself, an elderly gentleman and a duck.

At this point, the group of the thirty or so frightened people I had seen in the waiting room boarded the plane. They just stood there, wide-eyed, totally unaware of what they were supposed to do next. Cabin crew ushered them to their seats and had to spend a considerable amount of time reassuring them. I caught the eye of a flight attendant and asked her what was going on with them.

'They are from a very remote village, sir. They are being relocated near Kerala. They have never seen a plane before, let alone get on one. They live in the deepest parts of rural India. They don't understand technology at all, they don't have cars, tellies, nothing. I have explained that they can relax . . .'

I'm glad someone can . . .

'. . . and that the journey will be perfectly safe. I have told them that by road it would take many days to reach their new homeland, but this special machine can get them there incredibly quickly. In the blink of an eyelid. I'm sure you can see that they are very frightened and confused.'

'Absolutely. I know how they feel,' I said.

'One more thing, sir,' the attendant said. 'The captain has asked me to explain to you that we experienced a few problems with the brakes when we landed yesterday.'

Great.

'Because the runway where we are landing is much shorter than here, the pilot wants to initially do a test here. So he is planning to do an emergency stop first, before he decides if it's safe to take off for Kerala. Therefore he will make one run down the runway and then brake very hard, as if landing, to see what his stopping distance is. That's how he decides if it's safe or not.'

Interestingly the Air India curry was already deciding that for me.

'Thank you for letting me know,' I said unconvincingly.

The steward then told the newly boarded terrified passengers that they must put their belongings in the overhead lockers (those parts of the plane that had them). And so they threw all their belongings in these overhead racks and sat down. Those who had seat belts put them on.

Tightly.

I was now absolutely crapping myself.

As I have already mentioned, normally I am a pretty good flyer. After all, I've done so many trips over the years. But this was different. As the plane thundered down the runway, which incidentally had more grass and weeds growing on it than my lawn, its engines were *screaming* and I was gripping my seat for dear life. Even the duck shat itself.

Sure enough, halfway down the runway the captain slammed on the brakes and there was an almighty screeching noise as the bald tyres vainly tried to grip the runway. After what seemed an eternity, the plane shuddered to a halt.

At which point the thirty frightened villagers gave a huge cheer as they unbuckled their belts and proceeded to get their luggage down from the overhead lockers, ready to leave the plane. They'd been told beforehand what a special machine this was and how quick it was, but this must have totally freaked them out. Blink of an eyelid and we've arrived. Marvellous. They seemed mightily relieved.

It took nearly half an hour to settle them down in their seats before the captain eventually took off.

After a surprisingly incident-free flight, our plane eventually landed at our destination and we all disembarked somewhat relieved. As I walked across the runway to the terminal I looked back at the plane. Still, to this day, I don't know how it got off the ground.

I finally met up with the TV crew – it was just myself, a soundman, a cameraman and a director. Every day turned out to be different. Long hours and lots of travelling by road in rickety old vehicles of all shapes and sizes. It was a real adventure. I loved the people too.

Our first day found us on the actual spice trail itself. The director asked me to just walk along past these amazing ware-house full of spices. The mix of aromas was absolutely wonderful. I was loving it, despite my precarious journey down. Next on the agenda was to film a real snake-charmer. We found this really old and wrinkly man who must have weighed about five stone at the most, sitting cross-legged on the ground in front of a wicker basket with a lid on it. He had a long wooden oboe type of wind instru-ment in has lap. He was straight out of a film, only one tooth in his mouth and with a friendly/deranged grin on his face.

He beckoned me towards him and I bent down by his side and started speaking to camera. As I did so, the old man put the instrument to his lips and started playing. Quite beautiful it was too.

'Isn't this remarkable,' I began, 'this man here is playing a tradi-tional Indian wind instrument, look at the way he controls his breathing. You can hardly hear a break in the music . . .'

He beckoned with a nod of his head for me to get closer to him. I smiled at the camera and did his bidding. *This is good stuff*, I was thinking to myself. *The Beeb are going to be very pleased with this.*

I was really getting into it by now, leaning down towards the old man and his basket, describing the sounds, the colours, his body language – I was loving it.

Then the lid of the basket flew open and a bleeding great Indian cobra lunged out at me, his forked tongue no more than six inches from my face. They had to edit out my next word because this was a family show. I also added my own aroma in the air to that of the various herbs. I don't remember who reacted the fastest, me or the cameraman, but it's likely that neither of us will ever move that rapidly again.

'It was the shock as much as fear,' I tried to explain to my colleagues, who were desperately trying not to laugh. I found out later they had set me up.

The old snake charmer listened intently.

I continued with my explanation of both sudden movement and air pollution. 'I am well aware from reading up in books that the tourist snakes, such as the one we've just seen, have been treated so they are no longer poisonous . . .'

The old man grinned.

'No, sir, very poisony, sir, cobra bite you, you bloody deaded.'

We filmed everything from various festivals to princes' palaces to royal elephants, which was all just fantastic. One afternoon we stopped for a break and as I sat at a beachside café this little Indian boy selling scarves and a few trinkets approached the table. He was only a little kid and he spoke pretty decent English too, considering. He said, 'You buy? You buy?' I wanted to get something for my mum as it happened and I always like to buy local tourist stuff because it's only people trying to make a living. (In my previous literary outing, *Grumpy Old* . . . oh, you know the one. Well, I nearly ended up doing hard labour in Siberia for buying illicit KGB uniforms – if you still haven't bought the book by now, perhaps your local library might have a copy?)

I asked him how much for a scarf and then gave him a couple of notes, it was probably worth no more than a couple of quid. His eyes lit up and he ran off. The translator said, 'You needn't have paid that much, they expect you to barter.' I didn't mind, I felt good about the little episode and settled back into my chair to sip my coffee.

Two minutes later, the boy came back. This time he was carrying a sack full of stuff. He pulled out some hats. 'You buy? You buy?' Again we exchanged money and I now owned some hats as well.

Shortly followed by some belts, some T-shirts and a little while later some sunglasses. This kid must have come back about ten times. I tried to explain that I really didn't need anything else when he vanished once mor, only to return a minute later, slightly out of breath and carrying a plastic chair. 'You buy? You buy? Quickly please, you buy chair, very cheap!'

Before I had chance to say no, a nearby bar owner came running down the beach shouting, 'He's stolen my chair – stop him!'

After my second marriage collapsed, I returned from Switzerland to England with absolutely nothing. I was dossing in the spare room at Toby's girlfriend's flat – he was one of my road crew. Janet was really kind to me knowing I had absolutely nowhere to go and said I could stay until I'd sorted something more permanent out for myself. The flat was in Maida Vale in a building called Elgin Mansions.

One night I'd been down the Warwick pub, drunk a skinful and then gone for a curry. What is it about drinking eight pints of beer that makes a neon sign in your brain light up and flash 'I need a curry!'? There must be some neuro-scientific explanation for that.

Anyway, surprise, surprise, I had a vindaloo. Toby and myself staggered home sometime after midnight, and I walked in and collapsed on the floor. I never even made the bed! Next thing I know, it's early morning and Toby's missus is waking me up saying, 'Rick, there's a phone call for you.'

I pulled myself up from the carpet and stumbled into the kitchen. As I walked to the phone, I passed a mirror and caught sight of the full horror of my hangover. I looked dreadful and my breath smelled like a Turkish tram driver's armpit. I swear could have steamed wallpaper off from ten yards. I picked up the phone.

'Hello, Rick, it's Barry Norman here.'

Now I'd never met Barry Norman before, or spoken to him and my first thought was, *This is a gag, someone's pulling a fast one*, but as he continued talking I realised that it was Barry Norman. *How the hell did he get this number?*

'Rick,' he continued, 'I'm presenting a new series of *Omnibus* and I understand you've just done a new album called *1984* with an orchestra.'

'That's correct, Barry, yes.'

'Splendid. We thought it would be nice if you came on and played the overture for us to open the new series. Is that something you'd like to do? There's a three-hundred-pound fee.'

Three hundred quid was very much needed at that particular juncture in my life and so my reply was simple and straightforward.

'Yes, Barry, it is something I'd like to do.'

'Great, great. Also, Rick, we also wondered on the off chance if you might have a new piece of piano music that's not been heard before that we could also have you play, to counter the overture. The problem is the filming is in three days' time so it'll have to be a piece you've already composed. You don't happen to have a new piano piece, do you?'

I wasn't exactly in the best of positions to be writing and recording any music at all, as thanks to the last marriage break-up I no longer even owned a piano, so I was just about to say 'No' when Barry continued, 'There's another three hundred pounds in it, Rick.'

'Actually, Barry, there is a piece I wrote just a few days ago that I think would do the trick nicely.'

'Timing is quite crucial,' said Barry. 'How long is the piece?'

'How long do you actually need?'

'Three minutes and twenty seconds. Certainly no more than that.'

'Well, that's amazing, because this new piano piece of mine is exactly three minutes and twenty seconds long.'

'That's splendid, Rick – thank you so much.'

By now I was feeling rather pleased with myself. I had only been back in the country for a few days and already I was back on the television and earning a few quid to boot. My self-satisfaction and growing confidence was shattered by what Barry said next.

'And what is the name of this piano piece, please, so I can tell the producer?'

I was standing there in my underpants, massively hungover, smelling of a violent curry, head aching, with Barry Norman on the phone and I'd just promised to play a piece on national telly in three days that I hadn't even written yet. I was a mile away from having thought of the title. As I pondered my fate, I looked down and the morning mail was on the kitchen table. I looked at one of the letters lying there and saw the address written on the front.

Lightbulb moment.

'It's called "Elgin Mansions", Barry.'

'What a lovely name, Rick. I bet that's where you live. I can imagine a big mansion out in the countryside. I could see why that would be inspiring: you've probably got deer running round the grounds, a small lake, antiques everywhere, Rick, that's perfect.'

I wrote the piece the next day on a piano in the pub and went on the show and played it. Years later, I bumped into Barry while I was filming *Countdown* and he asked me if I still played 'Elgin Mansions'.

I told him the story of what had happened that morning when he called me.

'So you didn't live in a country pile called Elgin Mansions then?'

'No, Barry.'

'And the beautiful piano piece was not written about this place then?'

'No, Barry. It was named after the block of flats in Maida Vale where I was dossing on the floor and you can count yourself lucky that it was the envelope with the address on that I first clocked when on the phone to you, because just next to that letter was the receipt from the Indian restaurant . . . so the beautiful piano piece could well have ended up being called 'Tandoori Mayfair".'

There used to be two twin brothers who owned a fancy-dress hire and magic shop in the High Street, Slough. One of those brothers was the legendary Tommy Cooper who was, without doubt, one of the funniest people that has ever lived. Tommy had a huge following from the moment he broke into the business in the late 1940s, and his highly successful career spanned five decades until his untimely death in 1984. He was a huge stage and theatre star, his television shows attracted huge audiences and he even appeared in early comics in the 1950s. His shop in Slough was amazing. You'd walk into this big double-fronted shop and there'd be people juggling, doing magic tricks, there'd be a pantomime horse walking through – it was just so, so funny and a great place to go.

Whenever we bumped into each other, which sadly wasn't very often, Tommy and myself would always have a drink and a great time. They'd recently started a series of programmes called *An Audience With* . . . that was proving very popular. As you probably know, the audience is mostly filled with other celebrities so I occasionally got asked to go along to watch. They adapted it in later years so that some of the audience actually asked scripted questions, but in the early days it was just a celebrity coming on and doing their act in front of other celebs.

One of the shows I was invited to was to go and see the American comedienne Joan Rivers. She was just beginning to get known over here and was one of the few female American stand-ups enjoying success in the UK, so I was keen to go along and see what she was all about. Now, at any event like this you find yourself walking into the green room beforehand and immediately looking around for anyone you know, some celebrity that you can make a beeline for and start chatting to. I knew some of the faces from TV but not enough to strike up a conversation with, so I went and propped up the bar. Then, about a minute later, Tommy Cooper walked through the door, wearing a huge fake-fur coat. He scanned the room, saw my smiling face at the bar and wandered over.

He was with his lovely wife Gwen, and we chatted a little then Tommy said, 'This Joan Rivers – she's American, isn't she?'

'She is Tommy, yes.'

'I'm not going to get her humour, am I?' he asked, honestly.

'Err, no,' I agreed, 'I think probably not, Tommy. I don't get it all either, if that's any consolation.'

'I won't know when to laugh, Rick. I don't know why they invited me – I don't understand modern American humour. I don't know who this woman is but they tell me she's very big in America.'

'It'll be fine, Tommy. Just laugh when everyone else does,' I reassured him. Then the floor manager came in and ushered everyone into the studio at London Weekend Television on the South Bank for the live recording. Tommy, Gwen and myself were on the very back row which suited us just fine. As we sat down, a stagehand asked if Tommy would like to take off his fur coat – although it was a cold winter's night the studio was baking and Tommy's coat was just enormous.

'No, thank you, I'll keep it on if I may,' said Tommy, completely straight-faced.

We sat there and Joan started her act. She was very funny. However, Tommy clearly wasn't getting it at all. People were laughing around him, then stopping, after which there'd be a two-second gap before Tommy Cooper would start his famous 'huh-huh-huh' laugh. That made other people laugh, then there'd be another two-second gap and Tommy would think it was time to laugh again, so we just went round in circles. On several occasions Tommy looked at me and said, 'I don't get any of this.'

About twenty minutes into the act I could see that Tommy

was still not getting it. He leaned over to me and whispered in my ear, 'Do you fancy a drink?'

'Oh, Tom, I'd love one but we can't really leave our seats – it's being recorded live so we'll just have to sit it out, we can't just sneak out,' I said.

Tommy said, 'It's all right, Rick . . .' and with that he opened the side of his fur coat to reveal a full-size optic sewn into the lining, with a bottle of Scotch attached. Then he leant over to his wife and said, 'Tumblers please, Gwen.'

Gwen took out two fold–up plastic tumblers from her bag and we had one each.

'No ice, I'm afraid,' said Tommy as he handed me my very full tumbler of the finest Scotch whisky.

People all around started to look back to see what was going on and all around us the audience were in stitches.

I learnt so much more about Tommy Cooper and indeed many of the great stars that are no longer with us, from my dear friend Eric Sykes. I could tell the stories now, but I think I'll save them for the next batch of 'grumpy' stories.

'GETTING YOUR SHIT TOGETHER'

In 1972 it was the 'in' thing to go to the country and 'get your shit together'. That was the exact expression. Initially I hadn't really understood what this meant. I first heard the expression in 1971 in America, when some black dude, a really lovely musician I'd met in Los Angeles, was chatting with me about music.

'So, Rick, tell me: where do you Brits go to get your shit together?'

Way back then a lot of Americanisms that we now take for granted hadn't yet hit our shores so I really didn't have a clue what he was talking about. All I could think of was that in some way he was interested in gardening and was asking about manure, fertiliser, that sort of thing. So I just thought I'd play it cool.

'Oh, all over the place, all over.'

'Really?' he said, impressed. 'That's really cool. But surely you have a favourite place to get your shit together?'

All I could think of was Burnham Beeches in Buckinghamshire, because this was popular with gardeners who got peat and compost made from the rich, leafy woodland materials in that particular ancient woodland.

'Burnham Beeches, man, I often go there to get my shit together.'

'Cool – is that by the sea then, Rick?'

'No, it's in these beautiful, really old woodlands. Beeches spelt with two "e"s, named after all the beech trees there.'

'Wow, what a place to get your shit together.'

Exactly.

Eventually one of the Yes crew who'd previously toured around the USA put me right and explained the meaning of the phrase. Within twelve months, every self-respecting British rock band was going away somewhere remote 'to get their shit together'. You couldn't 'get your shit together' in your own home or round the corner, and you certainly couldn't do it at your parents'. I was eager to 'get my shit together' so I sat down and decided to buy a house somewhere in Devon. To get my shit together.

I bought this beautiful little farmhouse called Trevanin Farm in Devon, in a place called Woodbury Salterton. I loved it down there and spent an age 'getting my shit together'. People from London would ask where I was and the management would say, 'Oh, he's writing, getting his vibes . . . he's getting his shit together.'

Basically, what this *actually* meant was that I did the same as every other rock musician who was 'getting his shit together'. Bored with your normal surroundings, you told your management that you had some writing to do and needed to be somewhere away from the masses in order to get your shit together. The management would pass this information on to the record company, and basically all you did was vanish to your hidey-hole for as long as you liked, eventually return, having done nothing but get wrecked, and tell your management what great inspiration you'd had whilst getting your shit together. The management would then pass this information on to the record company that would inform the music press that you had now well and truly got your shit together. That's an awful lot of shit flying around if you think about it. I'm sure this eventually spawned the word 'bullshit'

For me though, it was important to get away from the pressures of being close to London and I just loved my place in

Devon. Now you might think that one long round of drinking with my mates in such wonderful hostelries as The Diggers Rest and the Alfington Inn had very little to do with getting my shit together, but it really did help me. I could relax down there. Go for walks with the dogs on the common or drive out onto Exmoor, spend a day at one of the seaside places such as Budleigh Salterton and generally just chill out until I felt ready to return to the madness of London.

Whilst in Devon, the press and media assumed I was discovering my music and rediscovering my inner artist. Many of my journalist friends were quite heavy drinkers and very often they would come down to see me in order to get their own shit together, which was nice.

Periodically an anxious record-company man would phone up.

'Rick, how are you?'

'I'm good, thanks. Still getting my shit together.'

'Okay. And how long do you think you will be getting your shit together, Rick?'

'Oh, it could be a while longer – there's quite a bit of shit to get together.' And off he'd go, satisfied that he had chased me and convinced that I was, at that very moment, working on some new masterpiece.

The beautiful part was that whenever I delivered a new piece of music, nobody ever had a clue where I'd actually written it and it was often assumed that Trevanin Farm was the key and so I was encouraged to go there a lot by my management.

To be fair, while I was down on my little farm I *did* switch off – the phone wasn't constantly ringing with managers, publishers and record executives chasing me every hour – so I did clear my head and feel refreshed. In fact, don't ask me how, but in-between the long drinking bouts of natural cider, I did actually write a large part of *Journey to the Centre of the Earth*, so perhaps I did get at least some shit together after all.

* * *

I spent a lot of time down in Devon and became friends with quite a few of the locals. I especially want to tell you about two of my favourites: Grizzle Greenslade and Jake Berry. Like many of the tales involving my mates in Devon, theirs begins in the Alfington Inn in the village of Alfington, near Ottery St Mary. Dave Cousins from The Strawbs had a house in the village, which he had bought a year before I bought my place as he felt the need to get his shit together twelve months before I did. So we regularly used to meet up at the Alfington Inn to get our shit together, together. We got to know all the locals and it was a fantastic place – I loved the Alfington Inn. It had old-fashioned table skittles, dominoes, all the old-school pub games. I was told recently that it no longer exists as a pub, so one day I may have to make a little trip down to south Devon to check for myself. Back in the 1970s, it was a real hive of activity and you used to meet the most amazing characters in there.

Like Grizzle Greenslade.

Grizzle had been brought up by his grandma in the village. He was a lovely, harmless fella but he was a little bit slow. He'd never really had a proper education and difficult circumstances meant he had to help his gran out round the house quite a bit, so the result was that he couldn't really read or write. All the guys in the village really looked after Grizzle: they made sure he had food and company and if the lads were going out they'd take Grizzle with them and then make sure he got home.

The Grizzle stories are legendary. For starters, he was not exactly tactful, mainly because he had little or no idea of social etiquette. For example, there was quite a pretty young girl who was the fiancée of one of the local thatchers and she was in the Alfington dancing to something on the jukebox one night. She saw Grizzle sitting on his own and felt a bit sorry for him.

'Would you like to dance with me, Grizzle?'

'I'd better not, thank you. I'd rather I didn't,' he replied.

Surprised, the pretty girl asked why.

'Because whenever I looks at you, it gives me the horn.'

She continued dancing on her own.

Grizzle had numerous jobs, which never lasted very long, and each and every tale of Grizzle's employment efforts has become folklore.

To his credit, he did try and hold on to jobs and was keen to pay his own way and stand on his own two feet – at various points in his life he'd worked for the council, most famously when he was painting the bridge over the little river at Ottery St Mary. One day in the Alfington Inn Jake Berry and Dave Cousins told me the story about Grizzle and how he came to lose his job with the council. Apparently, a van had lost control on the bridge, smashed through the railings and ended up in the water. It wasn't a long drop but the van was half on its roof and half submerged so the driver was obviously going to be shocked and frightened by his unfortunate experience. Jake and Dave were crying with laughter as they continued the story.

People soon gathered on the bridge and before anybody had even called the emergency services, Grizzle had run down the riverbank and wrenched the van door open. People started applauding.

'Wow, that's amazing – what a hero!' I replied, impressed. 'Saving the driver's life deserves some sort of award, I reckon.'

'Grizzle was arrested for grievous bodily harm,' said Jake.

'What! For saving a man's life?'

'Err, not exactly. Grizzle did pull the guy out, but then smacked him on the head and shouted, "You bastard! I've only just finished painting that bloody bridge!" then dropped him back in the water.'

Grizzle was let off the GBH charge but he did get the sack from the council.

Then he managed to get himself a job at a local golf course as part of the greenkeeping team. Grizzle loved his outdoor jobs, so we all thought this was the perfect type of work for him.

Within a couple of days, I heard a rumour that he'd already been sacked.

I saw him in the Alfington and said, 'Grizzle, what happened at the golf course? That sounded like it was perfect for you.'

'The bastards. They don't understand when you are just trying to help,' he replied cryptically. 'I just don't like it when you're trying to help and you get the sack.'

I said, 'Well, what did you do?'

'They asked me if I'd worked at a golf course before and I said I had. But their course was different to the one I'd worked at cos there were no windmills or funny obstacles to whack the ball through and this golf course was grass too, not concrete and it was far too big. People had to walk miles to find their ball after they'd hit them. Bloody stupid and they'd dress up in silly clothes.'

'Grizzle, where you worked before was crazy golf . . .'

'I know that now, don't I. Anyway, on my first day I had to start at seven in the morning. They gave me all these sticks with flags on and told me to go and put them on the greens, so I got the buggy thing with the trailer tractor and I drove on to these green bits where they wanted me to put flags in. I tell you what, Rick, it was beautiful, I've never seen grass like it. They were scattered all over the place so I just decided to find them one at a time. I couldn't believe it, though, right in the middle of each of these green bits there was a hole. I thought, *What a shame, they've done such a fantastic job and someone's left a hole there.* So I stuck the stick with the flag on the end in the ground – it had a spike in the end, you see, Rick – then I went round and filled up all these holes.'

'How many did you fill up. Grizzle?'

'Well, that's just it, Rick, there were loads, eighteen in all.'

It was actually a different kind of driving that Grizzle was most famous for. Because he couldn't read or write, it was very hard for him to get a driving licence. Impossible, in fact. This didn't stop him. He owned a blue Reliant Regal van. It was the same as the car in *Only Fools and Horses* which people always say is a Reliant Robin but it isn't, it's a Regal (and yes, I do play *Trivial Pursuit*). He had a Reliant Regal van because he could drive it on a provisional motorbike licence perfectly legally.

One day Grizzle announced he was going to take his driving test, so we all sat in the Alfington Inn trying to figure out how he could possibly pass and what we might be able to do to help him. Problem was that Grizzle was illiterate, like I said.

'That don't matter, does it?' Grizzle asked.

'Yes, it does matter, Grizzle. The first thing they will do is ask you to read a number plate on a nearby car.' So Jake had the bright idea of getting Grizzle to memorise his number plate. Then on the day of the test itself, the plan was that Jake would park his car right outside the driving test centre in the spot where the examiner usually pointed to a car to ask for the number plate to be read. Grizzle, having memorised the number could rattle off the number plate from memory while pretending to look at it and off he'd go to continue the test.

So it came to the day and he went to do the test. Jake drove to the test centre well beforehand.

Later that afternoon Grizzle stormed into the Alfington Inn effin' and blindin', having failed his test. Jake followed him in.

'Grizzle, what happened?'

'It was an effing disaster, Rick. It was all Jake's fault!'

'How was it my fault?' protested Jake. 'When I got there, I couldn't park in the space opposite so I had to park about half a mile up the road. Grizzle came out and the examiner pointed at the car opposite and said, "Can you read that number plate please?" and . . .'

Grizzle interjected . . .

'. . . And I said, "Nope, but I can read that number plate on that red car that's right up there at the end of the road." Jake's car was like a speck in the distance, Rick, but I said the number you all told me to remember anyway. Then the examiner said, "How do you know that? Can you see that far?"'

'And what did you say, Grizzle?'

'I said, "No, I can't see that far, but I know that's the number plate cos it's my mate Jake's car."'

'So you didn't get off to a very good start then, Grizzle,' I sighed.

'No, Rick, I didn't. But he didn't ask me to read any other number plates so we got in my Reliant. Then the examiner said, "When you are ready, Mr Greenslade, I want you to pull away, using all due care and attention to other traffic . . ."'

'And . . .?'

'Well, the nice lady at the hospital said the cyclist should be okay. He shouldn't be in there too long, and they let the driving examiner go home after they gave him some pills. I don't care anymore. I can drive my three-wheeler without anybody sitting in with me anyway so why bother to take a test. Can someone help me get the bicycle seat out of my front grill please.'

Quite a few months went by and I was spending some time at my house in Burnham Beeches in Buckinghamshire. I still had the Devon farm to 'get my shit together' but I was having a few days away from 'being away'. I was due to return to Devon to get some more shit together after the weekend and so I was packing my things in the bedroom when I looked out of the window at the long winding driveway screened either side with beautiful rhododendron bushes, through which were currently driving two police patrol cars followed rather erratically by a blue Reliant Regal van.

Grizzle.

They all parked in the drive and two policemen got out of the first car, then two more got out of the second car, then Grizzle Greenslade climbed out of the Reliant Regal. I opened my front door and said hello to the officers, only two of whom I recognised.

'Morning, Rick. Do you know this man?'

'Yes. That's Grizzle Greenslade.'

'Well, he says he knows you too. He's all yours.'

Grizzle stepped forward from behind the officers.'

'Hello, Grizzle, mate. What are you doing up here?'

'I'm on holiday, Rick.'

'That's lovely, Grizzle,' I said. 'Where are you going on holiday?'

'Here. Only took me six days.'

I looked at him in total bewilderment. The distance from Ottery St Mary to Burnham Beeches is about 170 miles. Even in a three-wheeled Reliant Regal it's only a six-hour journey at the most.

At this point, one of the policemen I didn't recognise spoke up. 'We are from the Berkshire police force, Mr Wakeman. We found Mr Greenslade lost in our area. Apparently, your friend tells us he can't read any road signs and he'd been stopping strangers in the street and saying, "Do you know where my mate Rick lives? He's in that band, Yes."'

The Berkshire boys had been handed Grizzle by the Surrey Police, whom in turn had been handed Grizzle by the Hampshire Police. Grizzle had in fact managed to reach my home from his home – just those 170 miles – via seven different counties and travelling just over 800 miles.

The Berkshire boys had traced where I lived, then they'd escorted Grizzle from Berkshire into Buckinghamshire because he was too much of a liability to leave roaming around the country roads.

'I like this house, Rick. Nice here, isn't it?' said Grizzle, blissfully unaware of the major police operation he was the centre of. Bless him, he stayed that night with us and we agreed we'd drive down to Devon early and make Grizzle follow us all the way right behind. I've never looked in my rear-view mirror so many times in one journey!

It's time to tell you about Jake Berry, another man I became firm friends with while I was in Devon 'getting my shit together'.

Jake was a real local character: he had this very strong Devon accent and mostly picked mushrooms and did odd jobs on local farms.

At the time, I was working on my epic *King Arthur* on ice shows at Wembley and as the production got bigger and bigger, I realised that I needed more crew, especially with the humping side of things (that's moving heavy equipment around for those of you with one-track minds). I was in the Alfington Inn and asked the lads one night if any of them fancied coming up to London to help out.

'I'll have some of that,' said Jake. 'I've never been further than Exeter before.'

Jake did indeed come up to work the show and he was *brilliant*. He really wanted to learn and he listened to everything the senior crew members told him. Most of my usual crew couldn't understand a word he said, but he kept telling me, 'Rick, corr, I love this, I wouldn't half mind doing this all the time.'

I explained to Jake that the only way to learn was by experiencing life on the road. If he really wanted to climb the ladder he would need to learn about drums, guitars, amps, PA systems, lighting, travel, management, record companies . . . the list just went on and on.

Shortly after, I had some shows in America and again I needed some extra hands. I suggested the idea to Jake, thinking it might possibly be too far for him to travel from Devon but he couldn't say yes fast enough. Before we set off, he did some more UK shows and started learning a little about being a keyboard tech, drum tech and so on. 'The only way you can learn is out on the road,' I kept telling Jake, 'and we're out on the road solid so you'll be able to learn fast if you want.' All the time he just kept saying, over and over, 'I want to learn, Rick.'

I have to say that Jake worked harder than anybody else in the crew and worked his socks off. He only had to be shown something once and he got it. We could all see that he was tailor-made for the business and would do very well. If only we could understand a bloody word of his thick Devonian accent then life would be complete!

The usual procedure with an American tour was to send the tour manager out there a week or so before the band arrived, to do what we called a 'recce'. He'd check the hotels were booked, the venue loading regulations, the equipment getting through Customs, setting up the rehearsal facilities, internal transport and working with the promoter and the agent to make sure all the shows were set up right – all the minute detail that goes into making an American tour a success.

Three days before the US dates, I phoned my manager Deal-a-Day's office and asked after the tour manager and his recce. Sandy, Deal-a-Day's secretary said, 'Well, we are a bit worried, actually, because we haven't heard back from him. We've checked the hotel but no one has checked in.'

'That's not like Toby at all. I hope he's all right,' I said.

'Well, we didn't send Toby – he was otherwise engaged.'

'Oh, so it's Big Ian. Still, I'd expect him to have been in touch . . .'

'It wasn't Big Ian either, Rick.'

'Oh my God, who did you send?'

'Jake Berry.'

'Jake Berry? As in Jake-from-down-the-Alfington Inn-I've-only-been-outside-Exeter-once-and-I've-been-helping-my-mate-Rick-a-bit-with-concerts-Berry? And he's now in New York prepping a major arena tour. With an accent as thick as Devon cream that's hard enough to understand if you live anywhere in England outside of Devon, never mind the Bronx . . .'

'That's the one.'

Great.

By this late stage we had little alternative but to fly anyway. The shows were booked so we decided to get there and try to salvage what we could from the wreckage. To my amazement, when I walked through Arrivals at Kennedy Airport in New York there was Jake Berry, waiting for me.

'Jake! Where've you been? We've all been desperately worried about you,' I said. 'You didn't check into the hotel and no one could get hold of you.'

'Everything's all under control, Rick. I've been staying with a mate,' replied Jake.

'A mate? In New York?' I said, incredulous.

'Yeah, he's a taxi driver called Enzo.' And with that Jake turned to his side and introduced me to his 'mate', who spoke with the broadest Bronx accent you've ever heard. Between them I don't think they knew a single word of actual Queen's English.

'Hi, Rick,' said Enzo. 'It's nice to finally meet you. This man Jake's funny.'

'Enzo's been great, Rick,' explained Jake. 'I got off the plane and Enzo was waiting in the taxi that I got in. I told Enzo where I was going but he didn't understand a word I was saying. He said he'd never heard an accent like mine. I couldn't understand a word he was saying back to me, though, so I showed him a map and he said, "You've never been here before, have you?" And I said, "No, I've only been further than Exeter the once for my friend Rick to do a show with him in London, on ice." Then Enzo said, "I'll show you around."'

'Show you around?' I asked, slightly alarmed.

'Yeah. First he took me to meet his wife, she's lovely, this real nice American-Italian, and she says "Why doesn't he stay with us?" so that's what I've been doing. He insisted that I didn't need to spend money staying at a hotel so I've been stopping over at his house . . .'

I could hardly believe my ears. I suspected my tour was already in total disarray and I'd probably never work in America again, but at least Jake was safe.

'. . . Anyway, Rick, Enzo has been driving me round while I've done all the recce. I have promised him tickets for Madison

Square Garden, I hope that's okay, Rick. It's all sorted, everything is exactly as the itinerary planned, I've had to adjust a few timings to make it more organised in a couple of places, but it's all done.'

I was completely stunned. And Jake was right. It turned out to be one of the most meticulously planned tours I've ever been on. Jake was a master at work. In America they loved him: the Devon accent made him stand out and his natural eye for detail meant he was a huge hit with everyone.

Jake worked with me for about four years and he tirelessly focused on learning everything there was to know.

Then he moved on and worked for AC/DC.

Then he got promoted and became an assistant tour manager. Very early on he was working with people like Michael Tait who is one of the world's foremost lighting designers, and Jake gained first-hand experience with innovative American sound systems and stadium shows.

Before long there wasn't anything he didn't know about touring.

Nowadays he still speaks with a strong Devon accent, which I'm sure is still cause for amusement . . .

. . . given that he is the very highly respected tour manager for the Rolling Stones.

I do love doing charity performances, but you can't do every one that comes your way or else you'd go broke very quickly. The problem is, no matter how many you do there are always yet more worthy causes that need help. It's quite frustrating at times, but there are of course only so many you can humanly fit in. Like most of the people I know in the entertainment business, I get about fifty requests a month to help out in some way. And the problem is they are always great causes. What most of us have are charities which we support on a regular basis and try and fit in one-off appearances for some of the others that come our way. Some of the really big stars get thousands of requests per year. You feel so bad saying no but the problem is that none of us have got infinite amounts of time and in order to cram something else in it would mean taking away your support from one of the other causes you already champion. I don't like being the patron of something unless I can actually take part in it. I don't see the point of having your name linked with a cause if you're not going to be properly involved. So it really is very difficult.

However, on occasion something crops up that you just happen to be able to slot in easily. Maybe there's a surprise evening off on tour or a similar break. One such request came into my office during the late 1980s while I was on tour with my son Adam. It was to raise money for a charity near St Ives in Cornwall and they had asked if I'd go down and do a concert. It just so happened that the tour with Adam was very modest and manageable, only a four-piece band and four crew, so I looked at the schedule – we had a day off that we'd lose but that was no bother – looked at the extra driving and so on and thought, *Yes, we can do this.*

The tiny theatre where the show was booked was run by a group of local people who seemed to have something to do with the church too. On arrival we were met by this very nice but completely mad woman. That's the kindest way I can put it. Very nice but very mad. She was in her fifties and dressed like a real hippie, with a flowing dress, kaftan coat, twenty-seven silk scarves and floated around like a fairy. As were all the people she was involved with. In the 1960s a lot of hippies had settled in the south-west and I guess some of these community-minded groups were still riddled with original hippies. It was like Woodstock all over again. I was quite relaxed but Adam was completely freaked out by them straight away.

This lady offered to take us to the theatre to look over the place, and as she opened the stage door we were met by the most overpowering smell of rotting vegetables. It was really violently pungent, eye-wateringly so. It was like being hit by a tidal wave of rancid cabbage. I was convinced that someone had died in there.

'What is that smell?' I gasped.

'Supper,' she replied. 'It's the cabbage curry,' she explained. 'As part of the ticket price, the audience will get a bowl of cabbage curry *before* the show starts. It's being made under the stage and the audience will be each given a bowl on their arrival.'

Now this venue was very small and certainly didn't have any air-conditioning, so the prospect of 250 people filling their bellies with cabbage curry before we walked on stage was not a particularly enticing one, even for a tour-hardened flatulent rock 'n' roller like myself. For Adam, all green round the gills and in his late teens, this was rapidly turning into his worst living nightmare.

'I want to go home, Dad.'

'Adam, don't worry, it will be all right . . .' I reassured him.

'Yes, but Dad – cabbage curry? And they are really weird people, I'm close to shitting myself.'

'Well, for God's sake don't eat the cabbage curry then or you really will shit yourself,' I told him. 'But try not to worry, we're here now, let's just keep our fingers crossed.'

So they let the audience in and fed them the 250 bowls of cabbage curry while we readied ourselves to go on stage.

Let me tell you that whatever smell you might imagine 250 people could make after simultaneously eating cabbage curry and then farting in a confined space is infinitely less offensive than the reality of what our noses were actually subjected to when we walked out on stage. It *stank*. It was horrendous. There was a near-invisible green mist that just hung in the air and the stench of the actual cabbage curry mixed with the effects emitted from the various rectums was quite literally suffocating. It was a good job we weren't reading sheet music because our eyes were streaming within minutes. It was unbelievable. Lee Pomeroy would have been proud (remember Costa Rica?).

We rattled through the concert pretty quickly, for obvious reasons, and right after the last note pretty much ran outside gasping for fresh air. One of the guys – Alan Thompson, the bass player – had actually eaten some of this cabbage curry. We didn't see him for another twenty-four hours.

After a few minutes, the mad hippie woman came outside and said how much everyone had enjoyed the show and thanked us very warmly. She then invited us to a celebration party in the church hall that was starting in ten minutes. By now Adam was like a rabbit caught in headlights: he was both genuinely terrified and actually quite mesmerised by the events of the evening. We got to the party and there were even more ageing hippies there, more original flower-power people.

The band and crew came and spoke to me as one.

'We'd like to skip the party please Rick, go back to the hotel, get rat-arsed, sleep for a few hours and leave at the crack of dawn. This place is barking.'

'I'm afraid we're all invited, chaps, so you'll all have to stay,' I responded.

It was not the most popular of statements and Adam was now sticking to me like a limpet when the mad fairy woman came over to me and said, 'We've got a present for you, as a small gesture of thanks for playing the concert.' I tried to say there was no need, dreading what they were going to give me, but she insisted.

I hope it's not a bloody bowl of cabbage curry, I thought.

'We have a poetry society, you see, Rick. And we even have our own poet laureate – he's called Rupert.'

'Right . . .' I didn't like where this was heading . . .

'And as a gift of thanks, Rupert is going to present you with one of his poems.'

Feeling relieved that I wasn't going to have to eat some of that foul-smelling curry, I said, 'That's very generous, thank you.'

She gestured towards the corner of the church hall, numerous silk scarves flailing all around her, and a man started walking towards us. I say 'man' – he was actually the closest thing to Merlin the Magician that I've ever seen with my own eyes. He was straight out of a science-fiction novel, with a long wispy grey beard, a black cloak and a pointed hat.

'Maybe it is time to go,' I said.

Rupert came over and a few adoring elves and pixies followed him, gazing at him like some kind of super-celebrity. Then the mad hippy woman said, 'This is a rare honour Rick, Rupert has never before given one of his poems away.'

I have to admit to being quite touched with this gesture as I am extremely fond of poetry and I was beginning to realise that what was about to happen was really something quite special.

And it was.

'Oh, that's really so very kind. Thank you so much.'

Rupert moved closer.

The elves, pixies and fairies all moved in closer with him.

I put my hand out, expecting him to give me the poem on some paper or beautiful scroll.

The mad fairy queen grabbed my arm and whispered in my ear. 'Rick, Rupert never actually writes down any of his poems. They are all works of art that he keeps in his head. They are only ever spoken, never read.'

I nodded knowingly. Adam and the rest of the band and crew starting edging toward the door.

I gestured for them to come back. They did so begrudgingly. Adam simply said. 'I want to go home, Dad.'

'It's okay,' I reassured him. 'Rupert is doing me the great honour of giving me one of his poems, not written down, but verbally.'

'I really do want to go home, Dad.'

'Shhh.'

The Fairy Queen continued. 'Rupert will now recite the poem and once he has spoken the words he will never utter the poem again: it will be a gift to you. It will pass from his mind to your mind.'

'Dad . . .'

'Not now, Adam.'

'How lovely,' I said. 'And what is the poem called?'

'"The Discontented Donkey",' replied Rupert, poker-faced.

I was already thinking, *How the hell am I going to remember this poem if they ask me to recite it back?* Then Rupert stepped forward and the elves and pixies made a circle around him. I was ushered into the circle to face Rupert. There was a pregnant pause whilst Rupert obviously was composing himself and then he looked at me and said, '"The Discontented Donkey", by Rupert.'

I stood expectantly waiting for a beautiful worded poem about a discontented donkey to come from his lips. I was mentally trying to work out how I would remember it, but I needn't have worried. It wasn't a lot to remember as he simply pulled his head back, brayed like a donkey and then walked away.

'Let's now go and discuss Rupert's gift to Rick everybody,' said the mad happy hippie woman. She headed off into a corner with a crowd of weirdos trailing her.

'Dad, I want . . .'

'So do I, son. Come on, let's get out of here!'

But before we could get out I was accosted by a very smartly dressed man in a pinstriped suit. He certainly didn't seem to fit in with the rest of the Happy Hippy brigade and so when he stopped to speak to me, I was not at all concerned.

Normality at last.

He spoke with a strong London accent and we got chatting.

'You're not from round these parts, are you?' I guessed.

'No, no, I'm a Londoner born and bred. I used to work in the City and that was obviously very stressful. I was in banking. Still am, in fact. I'm not married, I lived for my job, but it started to get on top of me, I worked ridiculous hours and I began to get depressed and had a sort of breakdown and so I came down here to sort myself out.'

'Ah, yes, to "get your shit together". People do that in my line of business too.' I said with a nod of the head.

'Pardon?' he said.

'Doesn't matter. Anyway, from meeting you now, this break away from City life certainly seems to have done the trick.'

'Exactly. More people should do it. I felt tremendous stress but coming down here helped me get my mind and body back to normality so I could return to work refreshed and raring to go. It certainly worked for me – in fact, next month I'm going back to London and I hope to take up a position similar to that which I left.'

'Well, that's marvellous. You should be very proud of yourself. And if you don't mind my asking, exactly how long have you been down here?'

'Just over thirty-two years.'

EPILOGUE

I will always try to sign every single autograph I'm asked for. This is all to do with my dad. Rewind to the early 1970s and I'm in The Strawbs. We'd just started to get a little bit of a reputation and had been booked to play Acton Town Hall. I saved enough money to take my mum and dad to a steakhouse afterwards because this was a big show at the time and I wanted to finish the evening by treating them to a nice meal out. The booking was for 11 p.m. which was when they took the last orders of the night.

The plan was to do the show, then Dad would get his car ready round the back with Mum already in there. I reckoned the show would finish about 10.30, so a quick change of clothing, rush out the back, jump in the car with Mum and Dad and we'd all race off to the steakhouse just before they closed.

Now, my dad was the most peaceful, kind, loving man you could ever wish to meet but this particular night was the only time that I ever saw him lose his temper.

Why?

Because when I came out of the stage door at 10.50 p.m., there were about two dozen people with Strawbs albums, asking for autographs. I signed about three or four but all the time I was looking at my watch, conscious of the risk of missing our reservation at the restaurant. After a couple of minutes I turned to the remaining fans and said, 'Look, I'm really sorry, I can't do any more,' and I jumped into my dad's car.

'Get out of my car!' Dad yelled.

I was so shocked.

'Why?!'

'You go back and sign every single one of those albums!'

'But we'll miss the restaurant.'

'I don't care. These people are far more important than a steak.'

Very sheepishly I got out and signed *everything*, then got back in the car and rather sulkily said, 'Well, we're not going to make it to the steakhouse now.'

'That's not as important, Rick,' said Dad, still visibly angry. 'Those people . . . you couldn't do what you do if it wasn't for them.'

We drove round to the steakhouse anyway and as luck would have it the manager let us in late and we sat down to eat. My father was initially very quiet, then after a while he put his cutlery down and spoke.

'Rick, I don't care if there are two people, two hundred or two thousand. If they've got something to sign, then you wait and sign the lot. How would you feel if you were waiting outside a stage door or football club waiting to get the autograph of someone you admired and when they appeared they just signed a couple of things and vanished?'

'I'd be pretty upset,' I said.

'Exactly,' he said. 'So in future, what are you going to do?'

'Sign everything, Dad.'

He smiled and things were suddenly back to normal.

Many years later, when my father had passed away, we were touring in South America. We'd just finished a big show in Buenos

Aires and down in Argentina, when you had played a big arena, they'd put you in a car right outside the stage door and take you back to the hotel very quickly, right past the waiting crowds outside. As we waited for the car, the promoter came in.

'Listen, there are a few VIPs who would like some albums signed Rick, if you could just do them, that would be marvellous. Don't worry about the rest of the people, there's far too many.'

The rest of my band understandably nodded. I didn't. I had this flashback to Acton Town Hall fifteen years' previous.

'How many are there?' I asked.

'Rick, there's at least two thousand people. Probably more. They're queuing all round the arena.'

'I'll sign them all.'

'Rick, you can't. It's insane, you'll never get through them all.'

'I'll do it.'

I know it sounds daft but right at that very moment, inside a dark backstage area of this huge arena in Buenos Aires in the early 1990s, all I could hear was my dad's voice. It was as if he was actually there. *'Rick, I don't care if there are two people, two hundred or two thousand. If they've got something to sign, then you wait and sign the lot.'*

My drummer Tony Fernandez said, 'I'll come with you, Rick.'

We didn't get back to the hotel until half past four in the morning.

I lay on my bed, absolutely exhausted, looked up and said out loud: 'Well, I hope you're bloody happy now, Dad. You always said I never listened to you. Well, Dad, I hope this proves to you that I did, and what's more, I always will. Speak to you tomorrow, Dad.'

And I did.

And I've spoken to him every day since.

LIST OF ILLUSTRATIONS

Plate Section 1
Page 1: Rick and Jack Douglas, © Doug McKenzie; Abanazer, from the author's collection.
Page 2: Heritage luncheon, © Doug McKenzie; Rick with Ian Freeman and David Graham, © Doug McKenzie.
Page 3: *Wot's on TV Tonight* tour, from the author's collection; Rick and Adam Wakeman, from the author's collection.
Page 4: Golf with Eric Sykes and Dennis Waterman, from the author's collection.
Page 5: Rick Wakeman, from the author's collection
Page 6: Benjamin and grandmother, from the author's collection; Rick with mother and Olive, from the author's collection.
Page 7: Golf, from the author's collection; Sound check, from the author's collection.
Page 8: Philadelphia party, both from the author's collection.

Plate Section 2:
Page 1: A young Rick, from the author's collection.
Page 2: With Robin Gibb, © Doug McKenzie; Celebrity golf, from the author's collection.

Page 3: With Ian Freeman and Robin and Dwina Gibb, © Doug McKenzie.

Page 4: Rick as a toddler, from the author's collection; Isle of Man fun run, from the author's collection

Page 5: With Wendy Richard and June Brown, © Doug McKenzie; Rick in Cuba from the author's collection.

Pages 6–7: Opening of Roy Castle Lung Cancer Institute, from the author's collection

Page 8: Cream bun fight, from the author's collection; With Adam Wakeman and Bonnie Tyler, from the author's collection.

INDEX